Contents

CHAP.	PAGE
1. THE SPIRIT OF TRUTH	1
2. THE EVIDENCE OF THINGS UNSEEN	21
3. THE ALCHEMY OF LOVE	48
4. THE HERITAGE OF PAIN	65
5. THE VESTURE OF GOD	91
6. SPIRITUAL CORRESPONDENCE	122

The Incarnate Purpose

I

THE SPIRIT OF TRUTH

THERE exists in certain religious circles the idea that criticism of Christian doctrine is an undesirable thing, because indicative of a spirit of irreverence and faithlessness that is at variance with the fundamental principles of Christianity. According to Catholic teaching, the Church is founded upon divine revelation, to doubt the reality of which is to question the truth of the Word of God. It is not to be supposed that the finite understandings of men can fathom the infinite mysteries of God. Does not the conception that it *is* possible for the divine truths of religion to be comprehended by means of the same evidential methods adopted in the acquisition of secular knowledge, imply a practical denial of the existence of a supreme God, since the creature would thus be made to appear as equal in wisdom and power with the Creator?

Most seekers after the Word of God meet at one time or other with some such argument against the propriety of their endeavours to obtain evidence of the intrinsic truth of Christian teaching. But the charge of irreverence brought against honest inquiry is powerless to affect the belief, held by many educated men and women, that a pure desire to know and to do the will of God necessitates the exercising of intellectual as well as of spiritual faculties, in order that what is true in the teaching offered to them in the name of Christ may be separated from what is false, to the greater glory of God and to the furthering of the divine purpose of Life.

Hostility towards criticism of religious doctrine appears to all impartial minds to be not only of doubtful service to the cause of Religion as a whole, but also to cast discredit on the ability of any particular creed to sustain an examination in detail of its articles. In an era when most things touching the health and general well-being of men are subjected to critical inquiry, it would be strange if their spiritual welfare should escape remark. Science has much to say about the food we eat, the clothes we wear, the habits of our daily lives; and we listen to what is said with due respect, because we know the aim of Science to be the improvement of the conditions of life through the elimination of error and harmful prejudice from the paths of progress; and because, by regulating our conduct by the reasonable principles recommended, we may contribute towards the amelioration of those conditions under which future generations of men will enter upon their inheritance of the earth. Is the authority claimed and exercised by the Church over the souls and minds of men to be unquestioned? Is the training of spiritual consciousness less important than the education and nourishment of the body? Scientific criticism may not be perfect, or its judgments infallible; but such as it is to-day, why may not its methods be applied to the elimination of falsehood and ignorance from things religious as well as from things secular?

The acquisition of knowledge has afforded throughout recorded history a perpetual basis for controversy on all matters which have excited sufficient interest or curiosity to command serious attention. It is difficult to think of any so-called natural phenomenon that has not at one time or other given rise to critical investigation, pursuit of which has sharpened the perceptions and widened the understandings of those whose energies have been engaged, and has thus contributed towards elucidation of the controverted subject. Especially is this remarkable in the declared differences between the exponents of scientific and religious doctrine. By reason of an intimate concern with the affairs of men, the methods of acquiring and imparting knowledge employed by the authoritative instructors of sacred and secular consciousness, offer an open field for controversy and challenge the criticism of all thinking persons. It will be admitted that the manner in which discussion is carried on, no less than the character of the conclusions arrived at, exerts an educative influence upon all questions of contemporary interest, so that, apart from the elucidation of Truth (which is the ideal end of controversy, but rarely its immediate outcome), an examination of the merits of conflicting opinions, or, in other words, a criticism of opposing opinions, would appear desirable if only as prefatory to the attainment of a more complete comprehension of the matter under dispute. The ultimate value of all such controversy is to a large extent determined by criticism, which acts as a salutary check on the tendency of most disputants to devote more attention to the question of who is right than of what is true; and where discussion is unattended by such restraint, a certain vagueness of purpose and procedure is apt to seduce controversy from the path of rectitude into a ramble among the byways of personal prejudice, which argues ill for the elucidation of the original subject under dispute.

But in considering the utility of controversy between the exponents of scientific and religious doctrine, it should be borne in mind that a victory accruing to either disputant can be of tentative value only unless and until its permanent worth be certified by course of time to be indeed demonstrated evidence of intrinsic verity. Until this is so proven the last word has not been said, although the path towards a more complete settlement of the point at issue may have been in some measure cleared of an impeding refuse of erroneous ideas and prejudices. Therefore verdicts determining the merits of conflicting opinions relating to abstract or speculative thought can rarely be regarded as final, and it appears unreasonable for either priest or scientist to resent as an outcome of controversial differences an issue favourable to his opponent, since only in the event of a subsequent endorsement of its intrinsic truth by inclusion in the commonly accepted facts of natural knowledge can the ruling of the judgment remain in force. Therefore, since the avowed object of both disputants is the elucidation of Truth, which process necessitates a concomitant elimination of Falsehood, neither priest nor scientist should resent such a satisfactory outcome of their contentions. For if the results of controversial criticism be not endorsed by the course of time, but are shown instead to be errors of judgment, rectifiable by succeeding generations of men whose advance in power of discernment is attested by the ability to eradicate from doctrine errors hitherto undemonstrable as such, the justification of controversy is even so sufficiently proven, inasmuch as its employment has brought about an expurgation of Falsehood, which accomplishment is, in the dual interests of Science and Religion, as important as the affirmation and confirmation of Truth.

A retrospective view of religious and scientific doctrine does indeed reveal controversy, accompanied by criticism, as a considerable factor in the evolution of knowledge, and its employment is clearly recognisable as a means of expurgating much that was false in ideas held in former days. It is reasonable to suppose that the same drastic spirit of controversial criticism so apparent in the past and so active in the present, will continue to operate in the future. But an examination of the controversial methods exercised to-day shows a remarkable change of tactics from those in use, say two hundred years ago—a change that is the direct result of the displacement of ancient weapons of war by modern arms. Evidence has supplanted the use of subtle verbal argument and carefully constructed syllogisms, whose premises were frequently contrived to corroborate foregone conclusions—a method not compatible with that earnest desire for truth above all things which is the war-cry of modern times. Evidence is everywhere proclaimed as the proper test for truth; and he who enters the field of controversy to-day, whether he be the champion of scientific or of religious doctrine, must, if he wish to obtain a serious hearing, come equipped with evidence of the truth of what he propounds, and with evidence of the falsehood of what he refutes.

This change in the method of controversial criticism affects all branches of learning, and is gradually bringing about a reform in educational matters that bids fair to shake the foundations of many lines of long-established conventional thought. Nowhere is the change more apparent than in the working of our schools. A child is no longer punished for asking the reason of what he is taught; lessons learnt by rote are a disgrace alike to schoolmaster and scholar. It is not the pupil who is impertinent in demanding, but the teacher who is inefficient and culpable if he cannot supply satisfactory evidence of the truth, the reality, the reason of his instruction. The kindergarten system; the elaborate construction of object-lessons contrived by means of illustration to exercise the child's reasoning faculties; the nature study, so swiftly establishing its place in the national curricula—all these are the outcome of the demand for evidence as the proper test of supposed truth, and are significant of the spirit of the age. Young people are encouraged to think for themselves; to accept authority only when there is evidence forthcoming of its right to be so acknowledged; to look for evidential testimony of all that they are called upon to receive as facts.

Upon the subject of education, Science and Ecclesiasticism are now engaged in what, seen in the light of after days, may well appear as one of the most important controversies of the age. And it is upon the very question of the fitness of evidence as a legitimate test of truth, especially with regard to the suitability of its application to religious as well as to secular instruction, that the chief difference turns. While Science, convinced of the efficacy of evidential testimony, employs the principle as a weapon of attack and defence in controversial warfare, the ambiguous attitude of Ecclesiasticism towards a similar mode of procedure places her at a hopeless disadvantage against her antagonists, deprives her of influence in most matters of intellectual importance, and stamps her as a deterring factor in the progress of the world. What fighting power, equipped with obsolete weapons of the eighteenth century, would be justified in hoping to meet with success in an engagement with a foe who carried modern arms?

If children are taught to regard evidence as a proper test of truth in matters of secular interest, and to disregard that principle in connection with their religious instruction, it follows as a matter of course that a line of distinction must be drawn between secular and religious education. It is regrettable that, interwoven as the two elements have been for centuries in the training of children, their division now seems necessary and imminent. Had they continued to work harmoniously together, the present differences between scientific and ecclesiastical methods of instruction might have been averted. But it is lamentably evident that in adopting an attitude of disapproval towards criticism of her articles, the Church is bringing about a division in educational matters that is becoming more and more pronounced. What kingdom divided against itself can stand? How can we expect to train our children in the ways of Truth if we give them no consistent standard for estimating what is true? How dare we hope to rear a generation worthy of its inheritance of nearly twenty centuries of established Christianity, when we formulate a religious standard of integrity in opposition to that of the secular knowledge of the world?

But it is not only over the Education Question that Science and Ecclesiasticism are virtually at war, although the conflicting principles underlying this controversial difference are illustrated by that dispute. It is not only children who suffer bewilderment by being asked to reconcile irreconcilable elements in their education. Both Science and the Catholic Church profess to be searchers after and upholders of Truth, yet year by year a chasm between them widens as their fundamental differences in procedure become defined; and year by year the number of honest thinkers who cease to regard themselves as members of the Church, or as under her authority, increases. So long as Ecclesiasticism continues to maintain an attitude of resentment towards criticism of religious doctrine, so long must this exodus of intelligence from the Church induce a practical development of the Christian ideals outside ecclesiastical circles.

It cannot be too vigorously affirmed that criticism of the pretensions of Ecclesiasticism is not necessarily an attack upon Christianity. Scientific research has never harmed or demolished the truth in doctrine attributed to Christ. Indeed, the simplicity and beauty of His teaching (in so far as this can be ascertained from a careful study of the Gospels) never shines so convincingly, and never exerts greater influence for good upon mankind, than when, under rational criticism, it is freed in some measure from the accumulation of centuries of superstitious ideas too long supported by the approval of Ecclesiasticism. Science has no quarrel with Christianity as such. A Christian Church, cleansed from all that obscures and dishonours Truth—a Church devoted to the practical furtherance of the ideals contained in Christ's Gospel of Love—would always have the ready help and support of Science. It is not from the Gospel of Love that men turn away to-day, but from dogmas antagonistic to reason, substituted for that gospel and taught by the Church as Truth in the name of Christ. It is not out of a spirit of irreverence that men demand evidence of the truth of what the Church offers them as Christian doctrine, but from an earnest desire to be faithful to that ideal of Truth which is surely the religious, as well as the secular, glory of life.

The figure of Christ stands as the centre of certain axioms professedly conducive to a right understanding of life and the right conduct of men, and He drew to Himself as supporters of His doctrine all sorts and conditions of men who became more or less imbued with the ideas of their Master. The accounts of His three years' mission which have come down to us in the present forms of the Gospels may or may not truly report His actual sayings and doings, and may or may not contain doctrine actually taught by Him. What is written, or by whom written, matters less than an assurance of its intrinsic truth when such is interpreted as doctrine applicable to the spiritual needs of men to-day. All that is true in the writings connected with the mission of Christ requires no miraculous accompaniment to demonstrate its truth: the only requisite standard by which its verity should be tested is that afforded from generation to generation by the current standard of knowledge. Is not the application of scientific methods of criticism to that grand conception of life and its responsibilities which we associate with the name of Christ, the highest compliment we can pay to His memory? For whether He really spoke certain words, did certain deeds, and taught certain doctrines, as in the Gospels He is reported to have done; whether He shared the errors of His age and is directly responsible for the introduction of teaching that is incompatible with known scientific facts; or whether He has not, perhaps, been made the scapegoat for the ignorance of those who came after Him—are questions of insignificant importance compared with the necessity for eliminating falsehood, by whomsoever spoken or written, from doctrine put forth as spiritual truth for thinking men of to-day.

In the estimation of many educated and unprejudiced persons, the fabric of Church government seems to have its origin in the perverted imaginations of men rather than in the ethical teaching of Christ, so far as this can be ascertained by a careful study of the books constituting the New Testament. Considering the discrepancies in the various sayings and doings of Christ as reported by the authors of those several books, the solution of the question as to what He really said and did becomes very difficult, and is complicated in all branches and phases of the history of the Christian Faith by subsequent accretions, finding their origins in the superstitions of the age, and for which no reasonable warrant seems to exist. We have, therefore, in an endeavour to reconcile the teaching of the Church with the supposed teaching of Christ, to fall back on the internal evidence of the intrinsic truth contained in His accepted sayings and doings. Acceptance of these as true occurrences depends upon how far they are consistent with established scientific facts. Truth is Truth, whether its unveiling to the understanding be achieved by Science or Religion. Investigation of the evidence of a supposed truth either, by certifying its verity, leads to its surer stability, with proportionate increase of honour; or, by tracing and eliminating error, gives higher value to the remaining purified residue. If the supposed teaching of Christ were found to be consistent with the modern teaching of Science, the mutual endorsement would be a further guarantee of the verity of the question in point, both in its religious and its scientific aspect. But if an examination of Christian doctrine reveals the presence of dogma utterly irreconcilable with known scientific facts, then, if the cry for Truth raised by both teachers is sincere, the rejection of that which defiles Truth is incumbent upon the disciples of Religion as well as upon those of Science.

The belligerent attitude of Ecclesiasticism towards criticism of her doctrine reflects indirectly discredit upon the Founder of Christianity. To bolster up falsehood taught and written in Christ's name is no honour to Him. The magnification of natural into supernatural occurrences, out of mistaken zeal for His glory, and the refusal to accept the verdict of rational investigation of the evidence for the truth of such occurrences, is not the way to further the ends of Christianity. Is it conceivable that the founder of a code of ethics calculated to meet the needs of men could desire exemption from an examination of the doctrine he taught and believed to be true, or, still less, of doctrine taught in his name, for the truth of which he has given no guarantee? Is it possible that Christ would have resented the idea of a future amplification of His doctrine on the lines of truth by men who perceived the spirit of His teaching, and who desired to honour Him by freeing it from its envelope of superstition, reflecting the errors of the ages through which it had passed? Did not He promise to men a Comforter who would abide with them for ever: "Even the Spirit of Truth, whom the world cannot receive, because it seeth him not, neither knoweth him.... The Comforter, which is the Holy Ghost, whom the Father will send in my name, he shall teach you all things, and bring all things to your remembrance, whatsoever I have said unto you.... When the Comforter is come, whom I will send unto you from the Father, even the Spirit of Truth, which proceedeth from the Father, he shall testify of me" (St John xiv. and xv.).

Did not Christ thus challenge the criticism of the future? Did not He plead for His teaching to be tested by the Spirit of Truth which, proceeding from God, the Father of all life, is present in the world as the guiding principle of all knowledge then, now, and to come? What is that sin against the Holy

Ghost impossible of forgiveness, but sin against the Spirit of Truth, which is a deliberate falling short of the glory of God?

II

THE EVIDENCE OF THINGS UNSEEN

THE difficulty felt in reconciling the idea of man's possession of an immortal soul with his supposed evolutionary physical descent is in many cases responsible for the exclusion of the scientific interpretation of life from the religious outlook. It is very naturally asked at what point in his development man obtained the spiritual faculty designated by the name of Soul, possession of which constitutes his chief claim to immortality. If he be indeed the product of an evolutionary process entailing the precursion and sacrifice of millions of generations of beings inferior to his present organisation; if his progenitors existed at some remote and unrecorded period of the history of the world, when distinction between man and beast was unknown, when did his separation as a spiritual creature occur? If some process of psychical evolution endowed him with a soul, may not other creatures than man, as yet insufficiently developed, obtain eventually similar spiritual attributes? How then, can the destiny of man be said to be superior to that of the beasts? Is there really such a thing as the soul? What are its distinctive qualities, and how is its presence in personality to be recognised? In short, is a belief in the immortal soul of man compatible with the evolutionary theory of his physical descent? If acceptance of the scientific explanation of his ancestry destroys the justification of his hope for immortality, is not life thereby robbed of its spiritual significance?

The history of mankind is a history of religion, wherein we may observe man's idea of the nature of God and of his own relation towards God, keeping pace with his development as an intellectual and spiritual creature.

When we review this evolutionary process, involving millions of generations of progenitors and covering immeasurable æons of time, we see emerging the creature destined to be known as man. With the slow dawn and growth of his intelligence, accompanied by a reaching out into an ever-widening environment, comes a dim perception of life and power outside himself—an acting force that is greater than his own. In apprehending the existence of God, man is evolved as a spiritual creature and stands in a kingdom of his own, destined to realise his essential unity with God as the Spirit of Life, in whose likeness he is made. *His apprehension of the existence of a spiritual God has given him a soul.* He sets about fulfilling his destiny. His attitude towards other organisms is that of Providence—of that Over-Lord who before his own spiritual birth was his own Providence, *i.e.* an active power outside himself and greater than his own. From this time forth his dominion is felt in the world as a governing force. His ability and authority increase with intellectual growth, until, as in the present day, the generation, development and extinction of species in the animal and vegetable kingdoms are to a certain extent modified by him according to his will and for his own ends.

Throughout his wonderful career we find his Deity representative of his own growing powers, and of his own attitude towards the governing forces of Nature. His conception of God is, in fact, the chronicle in serial form of his evolution as an intellectual and spiritual creature, a chronicle which faithfully records his progress and reflects his changing conditions of life.

A study of the religions of men of past ages is thus a study of the index of their lives, their thought, their social and moral status, enabling us to estimate their positions in the evolutionary scale of humanity. As we review this register of the life-stories of mankind, we find the idea of the nature of God keeping pace with intellectual advance. But although the distinguishing characteristic of man, even in his crudest stage, is always his idea of and his worship of a Deity, mankind as a whole has never worshipped at any one time the same idea of God. In the past as well as in the present, the many religions existing and obtaining credence and support all over the inhabited world give a fair idea of the intellectual and moral status of the people they represent. The ethical value of any religion is not gauged by an estimate of the number of its devotees as compared with those of any other religion. Its existence merely represents the mental state of those who are its adherents. As a rule, a religious creed is built upon a supposed special revelation of God; but to the scientist religions appear also as revelations of mankind. To him their value is retrospective and deductive, inasmuch as they offer evidence of intellectual growth, which he perceives to be the natural precursor of those spiritual conceptions of the nature of God which may become in course of time consolidated into dogmatic formulæ.

The extinction or survival of a religious creed as an active force points to the extinction or survival of that type of mind of which the creed was the reflection. Progress forbids uniformity of type and equality of structure on the spiritual as well as on the physical plane of life. Change and variety of religious feeling are necessary to the evolution of the soul, and should be welcomed as evidence of its growth. But not until, from the several types of man now inhabiting the earth, one were proved fit to survive in the struggle for existence and capable of maintaining its supremacy, could mankind worship the same idea of God. If this should ever occur, the change in the spiritual consciousness of man might be as stupendous and of consequences as far-reaching as that crisis in his physical evolution when the brute, becoming apprehensive of a God, was born into spiritual life and became possessed of a soul.

But the inequality of species cannot be adopted as the calculative basis of comparative virtue in the evolutionary scale, since the relative positions of organisms can only be determined by an examination of the degree of consciousness possessed by each in comparison with the others. For instance, although we say that a horse is a more highly organised creature than a rabbit, meaning thereby that according to our estimation he presents a more complicated mechanism, yet such a comparison of physical susceptibility is necessarily imperfect, because limited by the degree of our own discrimination. For since the correctness of our judicial opinions rests upon our ability properly to appreciate the true relation between intelligences and their environments different from our own, it follows that our criticism of their comparative complexity can be no criterion of intrinsic individual merit. The same inadequacy of human judgment applies to any attempt to estimate the degree of spiritual consciousness possessed by various organisms. Such endeavour may be successful in establishing a comparative standard for a rational criticism of religious creeds in their relation to physical evolution; but it is powerless to affix a stationary standard of morality to differently constructed intelligences.

The possession by creatures of faculties differing from those of others does not necessarily make for superiority or inferiority. That is to say, differentiation of type does not determine merit. A man is not superior to a horse because his structure and powers are unlike those of the horse; nor is a rabbit or a bird inferior either to a horse or to a man, since the organisation of all these creatures is adapted to different usage. Thus, the possession of a highly specialised brain does not in itself make of man a superior order of creation. The use or abuse of faculties, and the obedience or disobedience to the laws of being, offer the only standard by which the comparative superiority, inferiority, or equality of creatures of different organisation can be fairly estimated. And only by a similar comparison of the response to spiritual environment displayed by the followers of religious creeds can an approximate idea of their value be formed.

It is unreasonable to dissociate the evolution of any one organism from the evolution of the whole of life. All creatures have a common origin in the Spirit of Life, and if we believe that all things work together for good in the manifestation through love of this vital energy, all organisms are seen to be of mutual help in the development of spiritual consciousness as well as in the perfecting of physical form. There exists, therefore, no warrant for assuming that the physical and spiritual evolution of man is achieved more for his own separate good than for the common benefit of all forms of life; or that organisms other than man have not, or will never have, those spiritual conceptions of the nature of God which signify the development of what we designate as Soul.

Because all creatures are the works of God's hand—images of the Divine Will—evolutionary growth must surely bring them increasing consciousness of union with the essential Spirit of Life, which is at once the source and end of their beings. We are justified in assuming that the Creator does indeed draw from all His creatures recognition of an order dependent upon the manner and purpose of their kind. But though it be granted that perception of the presence of spiritual attributes in organisms may be resolved into an appreciation of the ability of creatures to conceive ideas of the nature of God, verification of any such supposed ability depends upon the standard of Truth upon which investigation is based.

Now, although evidence is rightly regarded as a proper test of all truth possible of comprehension, there may be apprehended the existence of infinite truths not demonstrable in their entirety, because their adequate expression necessitates faculties not possessed by the finite intelligence of man. When essential truth is in some measure perceived, it is always evidence that brings about comprehension; but when only dimly apprehended and shrouded in mystery, the intellect reaches forward into realms too hazy and undefined to allow of a deduction of evidential testimony in support of something not yet within the demonstrable scope of reason.

The ability to adduce evidential testimony in support of a declaration of supposed facts is essentially an artistic faculty, and a necessary part of the equipment of every teacher, whether he draw his accredited inspiration from religious, scientific, or artistic sources, if he desire to perform effectually his educational function. The work of an artist is the evidence of his art, by means of which he may promulgate his convictions and secure converts to his creed.

But while, comparatively speaking, few men set out to preach and teach some special gospel for the purpose of urging it upon their brethren, every man offers in his own person evidence of character which may become an educational factor in the lives of his fellow-men. We know and esteem a man by his works, which are the expression of his convictions and the fruit of his being. Without the evidence of virtue in the lives of those who profess to possess it, we are not justified in believing in its reality.

The artistic power of producing and recognising evidential testimony of supposed truths is part of the divine birthright of all men. The supreme Artist of Life, God, through whose works of art men may perceive the Spirit of Life, through whose creative energy the gospel of Infinite Truth is continuously made manifest, has given to man his body as a temple of truth, whereby the light of the spirit may shine out in evidence of its being. Made in the likeness of God, the handiwork of the Divine Artist, he manifests the glory of his Creator in his own human works of art—his creative powers witnessing to the essential divinity of his being. His senses give him evidence of his physical environment, and his reason, as the summary of sense, rightly seeks for verification of all that is announced to him as fact. But his senses cannot give him adequate evidence of his psychical environment, because its mere apprehension entails a transcending of the spirit over the medium of the flesh, thereby carrying vision beyond the point where verification of what is seen is possible, and where, attempting its expression, the vision becomes a shrunken incoherent thing, utterly inadequate as a likeness of what it is supposed to represent.

The poet, the seer, the musician, the sculptor know something of this inability to reach in their work expression worthy of its conception. And if this is so with the artist, how much more so with the genius, who is compelled by a force he does not wholly understand, and yet is possessed of some executive power of demonstration!

The genius lives in advance of his time, having a flash-like insight into knowledge hidden as mystery from the understandings of his fellow-men. He suffers the loneliness of the pioneer who, treading a path where none has trod before, leaves an open way with marks of guidance and explanation for those who come after him. But such a man has compensation for the lack of human fellowship in his consciousness of achieving work capable of raising the standard of thought in the minds of those who behold it. They may not understand, but they can admire. They acknowledge the work of genius— an attitude which is conducive towards a fuller appreciation of what they admire. They behold, in fact, evidence of something they do not fully understand, but which they apprehend to be true. Thus art fulfils its divinely ordered purpose in the evolution of the human mind, its educational influence being traceable in all records of human progress.

But there are spiritual ideals, visions of beauty, symphonies of harmony, unseen by earthly eyes, unheard by earthly ears, wholly impossible of demonstration, which remain for ever unexpressed and uncomprehended by those who have apprehended them. These seers of visions and dreamers of dreams have not, perhaps, the artistic power by which an attempt could be made to transcribe the vision in a manner legible to the ordinary human understanding. Or there exists, perhaps, no adequate evidence by which even a genius is able to express what he has apprehended in ideal and abstract thought. Yet to the dreamer, the seer, the genius an ideal is none the less true because he cannot certify its truth by evidence that would convey its verity to other persons.

One of the facts that the theory of the evolutionary descent of man and the evolutionary development of his soul has made clear is that there is no limit to his future acquirements of thought and understanding. Mental growth is a continual feeling after knowledge a little in advance of comprehension—of knowledge still hidden as mystery, to be approached only by a consistent application of the intellect towards the discovery of the evidence of truth in all things submitted to consideration. Speculative thought acts as an impetus to the mind to set about the finding of evidence that shall induce a natural growth of knowledge from mystery. Were there no knowledge inaccessible to the intellect, its development could not continue, for stagnation of thought, checking mental activity, must lead subsequently to degeneration. It is the effort to get, rather than the getting, which is the zest of existence. Without the hunger of mind and body, how could the nourishment necessary for the continuity of mental and physical life be obtained?

Truth is infinite, as God is infinite, and apprehension of this divine fact does not rest upon evidential testimony. But comprehension entails the evidence of reason, and is necessary to the evolution of the human understanding. Such evidence forms a link between mystery and knowledge, and offers a means by which the maturing intellect of man may obtain a gradual conversion of mystery into knowledge. Desire must precede fulfilment. May not the longing to penetrate ever further into mysteries not as yet, by reason of our imperfections, demonstrable to our intellects, be the pioneer of the discovery of truths now unknown, but which in the fulness of time will be given as the spiritual inheritance of all those who, being pure in heart, shall see God in a light of revelation that has kept pace through all ages with the evolution of mankind?

In such a manner does it seem that the desire for proof of human immortality should be considered.

It is difficult to conceive how, on the physical plane of existence, evidence of the survival of human individuality after death could be obtained.

The results of modern psychical research would seem to show that it is possible for the spirit of a dead person to be temporarily reinvested with a physical form other than its own body, and to communicate by this means with living persons. It is suggested that a spirit can so control a living person as to direct itself through him as a medium for some purpose not necessarily known to him. It is further suggested that, presupposing the survival of individual consciousness after death to be a fact, a disembodied spirit might so possess a living person with its influence as to become virtually reincarnate. It is known in ordinary life that the will of one person can so influence the thoughts of another as practically to annihilate his individuality, which, falling more and more completely beneath this dominating mental force, becomes finally a mere passive instrument of another's will. Is it not possible that this same domination of one personality over another, so often noticed in life, may be continued after death in an even more intense degree, and thus provide proof of the survival of individuality?

Unfortunately, although such hypotheses have been supported by psychical evidence and phenomena seemingly confirmative of their truth, there has been as yet no positive assurance that this so-called proof of survival of individual consciousness is not the result of telepathy either deliberately or innocently evoked from an extreme sensitiveness of the medium to the mental suggestions of those who desire to see the particular phenomena that are subsequently produced.

The Catholic Church asserts the possession of incontrovertible proof of the reality of human immortality, teaching that, unless the resurrection from the dead of the body of Christ be accepted as an actual historical fact, the Christian religion must of necessity become a vain and purposeless thing. But the evidence adduced in support of this doctrine is, from a scientific point of view, by no means conclusive. It is not, however, from Christian dogma alone that the hope of immortality has been born in the human breast; and justification for the reasonableness of that hope does not therefore rest solely on evidential testimony of the truth of the miraculous resurrection of Jesus Christ.

Although it would seem that the survival of individual consciousness after death, whether it be attested by a possible spiritual reincarnation, or whether by the Christian doctrine of the Resurrection, cannot be regarded as assured by any evidence satisfying the requirements of scientific criticism, yet we are not therefore justified in assuming that confirmation of the reality of these spiritual apprehensions of human immortality will be for ever withheld from the human understanding. Man, being capable of foreseeing death as an inevitable termination of his earthly existence, has conceived the idea of spiritual survival as a possible corollary of physical life. But for the justification of this hope there is as yet no conclusive evidence, since demonstration of its truth necessitates a transference of thought from the finite reckoning to that of Infinite Truth veiled as yet in mystery.

A creature which by reason of its organisation lacked the intellectual capacity to imagine its death, could not know the desire for immortality. Before man arrived at that stage in his evolution when he was able to foresee his death as an inevitable occurrence, we may suppose that he knew no craving for life after death. But the instinct of self-preservation, common to all forms of life, becomes in him the natural precursor of the hope of immortality—that spiritual desire which gives a special and divine character to humanity. That intellectual development which gives the capacity to foresee the inevitableness of physical dissolution is thus responsible for the apprehension of a spiritual survival of death. Recognition of the truth that the life of the world continues after the individual has suffered physical death carries with it some consciousness of the circulation of other vital force. Knowledge of death is thus preliminary to man's perception of the continuity of life, and a necessary preparation for his acquisition of such consciousness of impersonal vitality as leads to his apprehension of a Spiritual God, whence he perceives his own vitality to be derived. With recognition of God as the Divine Spirit of Life, his hope of immortality is justified of its conception. For if the life of God be in man, his spirit cannot die. Is not this self-knowledge the spiritual birthright of all men, to which Christ referred in the words, "Except a man be born again, he cannot see the kingdom of God" (St John iii. 3)?

Out of a knowledge of death, consciousness of spiritual life is evolved, from which springs the desire for immortality. "Since by man came death, by man came also the resurrection of the dead" (1 Cor. xv.).

The evolving intellect of man has given him knowledge of the inevitableness of death as the termination of physical existence, and from this evolution of intellect is born the spiritual apprehension of the resurrection of the dead—of that immortality of the Divine Spirit of Life which is the veritable essence of the teaching of Christ, and which finds endorsement in the modern scientific interpretation of the laws of Nature. Does not the evolutionary theory of the descent of man, by showing his spiritual development to be in accord with the scientific explanation of his origin, endorse the words of Christ relating to his spiritual inheritance of immortality?

Hope, the outcome of the imaginative or creative faculty in man, is the pioneer of knowledge, for it is by that reaching out of the human mind into realms of speculative thought that ideas and apprehensions, if true, become gradually clothed with evidence of their truth, according as the spiritual and physical evolution of man makes him more capable of approaching the illimitable and infinite glory of God.

The self-education of a child is achieved by a continual process of verification of his speculative thought by evidence. His ideas are regulated by the evidence he can deduce capable of realising them, when they are instantly registered as experience, which forms an ever-broadening base for further speculative flights of the imagination. As the mind matures, this faculty of speculative thought becomes, under the name of initiative, the germ of all undertakings calling for personal direction and action. A man undertakes to do certain things because he has confidence in his executive powers. He has experienced the evidence of his capability and verified his powers, and he therefore dares to go boldly forward into wider fields of action. A child still crudely experimenting for evidence of the truth of his own small infantine powers of apprehension, has as yet no conception of yet vaster knowledge awaiting his more matured mind. The knowledge and power possessed by his father are a mystery to him, calling forth his respect and awe, so that he scarcely dares to think he may one day be as wise himself.

The knowledge of God and of Infinite Truth which a man has not in its completeness is a mystery to him, calling forth his respect and awe as his own powers inspire his little son with a like veneration. But nothing forbids a man from changing the mystery of God into a knowledge of God, *if he have understanding capable of meeting the revelation,* just as there is nothing to forbid a child from making the mystery of his father's knowledge his own possession if he have adequate power of comprehension.

Evidence *is* a proper test of all truths possible of comprehension, but it is no test of the existence of Infinite Truth, by which the world and the affairs of men are formed for a purpose withheld as yet in its entirety from the imperfect human understanding.

Where it has been given to man to penetrate some way into the knowledge of so-called Natural Law, a beautiful coherency in the structure and continuity of life has always been observed. The Unity of Nature, and the working together of the Whole of Life, is a fact, the evidence of which has been deduced and declared over and over again in corroborative detail as the results of scientific investigation. Could the history of the intellectual attainments of man be to-day unrolled before his wondering gaze, there would, we are told, appear no break in the perfect continuity of his ascending life, but instead a perpetual adjustment of the evidence of his speculative thought—of evidence so contrived as to keep pace with his capacity to understand. And could his future history be in a like manner revealed to him to-day; could he foresee that mysteries, now so incomprehensible, are yet destined to be comprehended by him as knowledge, we are justified in believing there would appear the same beautiful coherency in his spiritual evolution which has marked his material progress in the past.

When man is ready to receive the verification of the immortality he hopes for, but for which he has as yet no scientific evidence, we may be sure it will be given to him. Signs are not wanting that this almost universal craving of the human race is not to remain for ever unsatisfied. Meanwhile, can we not watch one hour? The day is certain when we shall all in our own persons receive confirmation of the truth of our apprehensive hope for immortal life. Can we not, then, in acquiescence with the Will of God, which all experience teaches us to be a directing Will for Good, rest content in the belief that because evidence of a truth is never withheld from those capable of understanding it, so we, when we are ready for a verification of this desire of the soul, may be given the evidence for which we hope?

III

THE ALCHEMY OF LOVE

ONE of the most perplexing and saddening problems of life, which presents itself in mournful frequency to thoughtful minds, is that of so-called unmerited suffering. This seeming injustice, co-operative throughout Nature with the struggle for existence, is a stumbling-block to many thinkers to whom the creed of propitiation for sin and suffering in the person and mission of Christ, as well as those dicta of Natural Science which declare the sacrifice of the weak and helpless to be a necessary accompaniment of evolutionary life, appear rather as different aspects of vicarious suffering than as reconciliating explanations of its compatibility with the supreme government of a God of Love. Is it not the fact that a large proportion of our trouble and perplexity concerning certain problems of spiritual morality has origin in our resentment at the seeming injustice of the operation of the law of suffering? In grief and sadness of heart we cry out against the infliction of sorrow and pain upon those who are made to suffer vicariously for the wrong-doing of others. Surely a God who wreaks vengeance for one man's sin upon his innocent children cannot be a God of Justice! Surely the dealing out of madness as the reward for superlative endeavour, strenuous idealism of thought, and consistent self-denial, the inflicting upon finely organised sensitive temperaments a capacity to suffer in a measure scarcely appreciable by coarser natures, cannot be by the direction of a God of Love! When we behold the visitation of such mental and physical torture upon pure and upright men and women, whose conduct seems utterly undeserving of punishment, we ask ourselves if such things can be in accord with the supreme government of Divine Love. Our hospitals and asylums are recruited largely from the ranks of those who suffer from the wrong-doing of others. Inherited disease and tainted environment set from birth a handicap tantamount to foredoomed life-failure upon the children of the multiplied unfit, whose continued tenancy of the earth constitutes a deterring factor in progressive life. If these things are done by divine ordinance, surely the laws of human justice, framed for the punishment of wickedness and vice, and for the maintenance of virtue and its reward, are more in accord with a true conception of a government of Love and Justice! Can it truly be the Will of God that the innocent shall suffer for the guilty, the pure for the impure, the just for the unjust? If so, for what end are these things ordained?

Most of us have at one time or other "withered and agonised" under the relentless insistency with which some such ideas as these have intruded upon our spiritual tranquillity. We try to put them aside as beyond our understanding. We tell ourselves that we lack faith, that we are not meant to comprehend the mysteries of God. And yet, if the Creator endows His creatures with the ability to question, and thus approach, the border-land between Known and Unknown, Seen and Unseen, can it indeed be irreverent or presumptuous to look to Him for guidance from mystery into knowledge, from ignorance into understanding?

If the revelation of God be indeed a revelation throughout Nature, chronicled by the evolving collective consciousness of Creation; and if the incarnate purpose of Love be recognisable as the vesture of the Spirit of Life, God; can a like unfolding of the Will of Love be withheld from personal and individual understanding?

It is clear that problems of spiritual morality must be approached from the spiritual plane of thought. That which pertains to the manifestation of spiritual consciousness and which is subject to the time-limit of human calculation must be dissociated from apprehension and contemplation of the eternal verities. If we would regard life as a Whole, and thus attain a right appreciation of the relation of individual consciousness to spiritual unity, we must learn to live in the Whole. If we desire a true understanding of the government of life; if we would conduct aright our critical inquiry into the methods by which the law of suffering manifests the progressively revealed Will of Love; if we would behold this Will of Love pictured upon the face of life, and receive the same spiritual illumination upon our souls, we must first establish a right attitude of heart and mind towards the divine revelation.

Differences noticeable between the religious and scientific interpretations of certain phenomena are not necessarily fundamentally hostile the one to the other, since each represents an opposing point of view rather than a contradictory likeness of fact. Any system of reflective thought, registered as opinion and propagated as substantial truth, may appear in opposition to any other established line of thought; but neither should be on this account judged as wholly right or wholly wrong, since each may be a perfectly correct impression of the thing seen, if the reflective machinery available has been properly employed. For whether artistic perception be utilised as an aid to the desire so to interpret Nature as to provide an endorsement of psychical apprehension, or whether it be directed towards the production of evidence for the verification of intellectual conjecture, the alternative result of a religious or a scientific interpretation of life is equally dependent upon focus for its representation in kind.

Under certain unlike conditions of light and distance, two artists engaged in the representation of the same object produce totally different impressions of the thing seen. Difference of focus in the actual outward vision; difference of personality, whereby difference in the mental powers of registration, reconstruction and expression becomes apparent, are together productive of difference in representation. A discerning critic does not, however, condemn either picture as worthless or incorrect because the one does not resemble the other. He knows that a just opinion of their respective values rests upon his ability to gauge that relative difference of focus which is responsible for their dissimilarity. The worth of his criticism depends upon his capacity so to focus his own point of view as to embrace and reconcile the differences of aspect in the representations submitted to his judgment. Given this ability, he is aware that his perception of the reconciled differences has enlarged his own appreciation of what he is called upon to judge. His criticism becomes his own enlightenment. Thus it appears that true critical appreciation is based upon the focussing of diverging points of view into converging actuality; and only when inquiry is attended with such impartial discernment can elucidation ensue.

The question of suffering, particularly of vicarious suffering, is one which, from the intimate nature of its bearing on the spiritual as well as on the physical aspect of human consciousness, gives rise to certain apparent irreconcilable differences between the religious and the scientific interpretation of its place and meaning in the scheme of life. On the one hand we have the point of view derived from that type of mind which cannot dissociate suffering from sin, regarding each as a concomitant consequence of a derangement of the divine and originally perfect order of Creation by reason of the intervention of Evil in opposition to God's Will for Good. Such is the creed of pessimistic suffering—a practical denial of the progressive action of the Spirit of Love. On the other hand, there is the point of view derived from that type of mind which believes the susceptibility of organisms to contrasting sensations to be a necessary factor in spiritual as well as in physical evolution. Such is the creed of optimistic suffering—the affirmation of the inherence of the divine Spirit of Life in all creatures, whereby pain and evil are shown to be as truly ordained by God as those opposing elements of consciousness known to us as joy and good, to the end that for evil so much good more, for sorrow so much joy more, may be evolved through the transmuting and progressive purpose of His Will.

Here, then, are two aspects of the phenomenon of suffering—two pictures of life drawn from two points of view—the one apparently so irreconcilable with the other as to make it difficult to realise that it is indeed one and the same objective which is subjected to critical inquiry, *i.e.* the compatibility of sin and suffering in a world created and controlled by a God of Love. But we are not justified in condemning, on the score of dissimilarity of conception and treatment, either representation as incorrect or worthless. The point of focus is responsible for their seeming contradiction. May not, therefore, some adjustment of our powers of critical discernment give us a point of focus which shall embrace both aspects, reconcile their seeming contradictions and differences, and enable us to draw one comprehensive conclusion from them both, to the enlightenment of our intellectual and spiritual consciousness? Our analytical appreciation is directed towards a fair consideration of different aspects of a natural phenomenon. Is it not possible to attain a vantage-ground above the divergence of aspects high enough to allow us to behold the spiritual and physical signification of suffering as one harmonious accompaniment of spiritual and physical evolution, in accord with the divine directing Will of Love?

As, within the physical universe, sound-waves, once set in motion, must circulate for ever, ripple on ripple, in widening vistas of echoing reproduction, unless broken in their course by contact with some barrier capable of arresting and absorbing the progress of vibration; so, in spiritual consciousness, the influences for good and evil which emanate from all effort, whether individual or collective, volitionary or involuntary, must circulate for ever throughout Infinity, unless checked, broken, absorbed, cancelled by centralization in some interposing and receptive agent. And so, within the Communion of Love, the saints on earth, chosen by God as worthy to co-operate in the divinely appointed regenerating purpose of life, may summarise and transmute the effects of evil into good by means of their own suffering; may so sanctify their minds and bodies as temples of the Holy Spirit, that they may be found worthy to share the passion of Incarnate Love in the redemption of the world. It is the Will of God, it is the Law of Life, that we bear each other's burdens; that the just suffer for the unjust, the innocent for the guilty, the pure for the impure! Not in ourselves or by ourselves alone can sins of commission and omission be expiated; not by our own unaided efforts can we arrest the consequences of action. Life is a whole, and individual thought and action touch the whole, and their effects are felt by the whole. We derive no virtue in ourselves from ourselves alone. Do we not owe our very ability to discriminate between good and evil, our standard of right and wrong, our civilization, our culture —nay, in short, the whole of our evolving realization of the Love of God— to the collective consciousness of Creation, which is a continual revelation of God? Do not we stand to-day as inheritors of wisdom accumulated by the united efforts of mankind in past times, and as guardians of this, the world's increasing consciousness of God, revealed throughout all Time, throughout all Creation? According as our forefathers struggled and attained, do we in our generation enter upon the inheritance of the earth. Thus the progressive spiritual consciousness of the world is at once our inheritance and our trust. We are debtors to the past and custodians of the future generations of our kind. Through the infinite condescension of God in employing mankind as a medium of His revelation, the privilege of realising the increasing purpose of His Will is placed within our keeping. Made in the image of God, man is endowed with the creative faculties of his Maker. The Creator wills that His creatures shall consciously share in the glory of creation, whereby through the perfecting of spiritual apprehension is revealed the Kingdom of God. Are we willing to take up the cross of sacrifice and suffer gladly with and in the passion of Incarnate Love? If we are indeed judged worthy of use in the elimination of evil by conversion through suffering of the effects of evil into elements of good, must we not rejoice in our participation with Divine Love in the revelation of the glory of God? If we are called upon to surrender ourselves, our minds and souls and bodies, as a reasonable sacrifice in the service of Love; if we are chosen by God to suffer in Love and with Love in the progressive redemption of the world from evil by the translation and transmutation of its effects in ourselves through suffering into recreated good; shall we not uplift our hearts and minds and souls in praise, prayer and thanksgiving, in that we are thus consciously brought into the Holy Communion of Love?

All creation groaneth and travaileth together, but it is not given to all forms of life to suffer consciously and willingly in co-operation with the divine government of life. Participation in the redemption and salvation of the world through Love is the privilege of those only who are born into spiritual apprehension of their essential unity with God, and who thus become one with Him in the transmuting purpose of His Will. These are they who, obeying the command of Love to resist not evil, become agents of the divine Alchemist. But the power thus to suffer willingly in the transmuting process of spiritual progress implies a dual susceptibility of physical and psychical consciousness which is the peculiar privilege of mankind. The whole organic world lies under that law of suffering which ordains that the sacrifice of individual interest shall form the collective and increasing good of life. But to humanity alone as yet has been given perception and power to share consciously in the divine government of Creation. As part of the organic world we are bound by the law of suffering, but we are not condemned to suffer in total ignorance of the purpose behind the working of the Will of God. We are spiritual beings, made in the image of God, and endowed with a birthright of free-will. We are called upon to suffer *gladly* in Love and for Love, so that the Creator may be glorified in His creatures. We are chosen instruments of the divine Will, but we are free to accept or refuse our election into active service in the Communion of Love. Shall we give ourselves to God in willing co-operation with the divine regenerating purpose of life? Or shall we resent the sacrifice of ourselves in the forwarding of His Will? We are offered co-operation with the Spirit of Life, whereby we may become the agents of divine healing in the progressive redemption of the world, and whereby the effects of evil may be transmuted into elements of good. We are called upon to share the passion of Incarnate Love and to take up *willingly* the cross of sacrifice. If we disregard the divine command to suffer gladly, we reduce ourselves to the level of the unenlightened brute creation, thereby proving ourselves unworthy of our vocation to conscious and active membership of the Communion of Love, inasmuch as we stultify the divinely implanted powers of transmutation and redemption within us, and hinder the coming of the Kingdom of God on earth.

For, if men are responsible to a certain extent for their own suffering and disease of mind and body; if payment in their own persons is exacted as a just result of ignorance, or as the punishment of abuse of knowledge; yet the consequences of thought and action are not thereby entirely arrested. Life is a Whole, and the conduct of the members of the spiritual Communion of Love must affect the Whole for evil or good. By our willing acceptance of our suffering as the transmuting agent for the conversion of the effects of ignorance and of active evil into elements of recreated good; by our endeavours to add to the world's accumulating consciousness of the Love of God by means of our own rightly directed thought and action; by our readiness to suffer in ourselves the physical and psychical effects of evil, and translate them into good, may we not prove ourselves more worthy of our high vocation to the Communion of Love?

IV

THE HERITAGE OF PAIN

In the foregoing pages has been set forward some attempt to explain how the transmuting action of the creed of optimistic suffering operates in a progressive revelation of the spiritual unity of the Whole of Life, whereby pain appears as the agent of the Will of a God of Love in the conversion of evil into good, and whereby the perfecting consciousness of Creation may be drawn into willing co-operation with the Creator.

Such an interpretation of the presence of evil and pain in the world is in agreement with that advanced by Science in support of the supposition that evolutionary growth entails the susceptibility of organisms to contrasting sensations. But is it also compatible with that other explanation of the origin of evil which holds the sin of Adam accountable for the suffering of the whole world, and upon which is based the ecclesiastical doctrine of the need of the Christian Atonement?

While affirming the interdependence of sin and suffering, there is drawn a careful distinction between the two, observation of which is necessary by the man who would avail himself of the Church's aid in the salvation of his soul. Supported as allegorical truth, if not as actual historical occurrences, the Hebrew legends of the Creation and the Fall have been adopted as an explanatory foundation for the need of a new covenant between man, whose sinful conduct marred an originally perfect world, and his justly offended Deity.

Before the advent of Christ the souls of men are held to have been in bondage to the spirit of evil. But through the death of Christ the wrath of God was appeased, and redemption of the sins of all who should acknowledge His redemptive power was secured.

The Catholic Church, as the accredited representative of the divine authority of Christ, teaches that by sacramental agency men may obtain remission and absolution of sins. But there is no concomitant remission of suffering, which is the consequence of evil-doing. The painful labour of men and the travail of women are the result of sin committed by their progenitors, Adam and Eve. It is one thing to forgive a wrong action, but another to arrest its mischievous effects. Man, having marred God's scheme of Creation, must suffer to the end of time from the ineradicable presence of evil in the world, although individual responsibility for its existence is secured by belief in the power of absolution claimed by the Catholic Church in the carrying on of Christ's mission of redemption.

Ecclesiasticism hails Christ as the Saviour of the world, inasmuch as His death was a sacrifice sufficient to atone for the sins of all men. But it is reserved for Science to confirm the truth of this spiritual recognition of the Divine Redeemer, Love, by evidential testimony adduced from proven facts of so-called natural law, whereby Christ is seen as the expounder of doctrine that controverts the theory of evil and suffering as opposing forces to the Will of a God of Love, and reveals their purpose in the spiritual evolution of mankind.

To the scientific mind, sin is non-existent apart from recognition of moral law. Reason asserts that a knowledge of evil is necessary to a knowledge of good, discrimination between the two being preliminary to the establishment of moral law; that such discrimination is chiefly obtained through the sensibility of organisms, the degree of whose susceptibility determines their relative positions in the evolutionary scale—a degree which terminates in man, who manifests the highest consciousness, estimated by his ability to feel, and the highest form of intelligence of any known creature.

Although sensory consciousness may be regarded as a register by which the relative positions of organisms in the evolutionary scale may be determined, the increasing inability to speak positively with regard to distinction between living and non-living matter forbids any dogmatism as to the impropriety of applying the term "conscious" to the inorganic world.

It is, perhaps, here permissible to suggest a possible point of reconciliation between the natural desire of men to obtain evidence of their spiritual survival of organic decay and that disregard of individual importance and advantage which is characteristic of a purely secular interpretation of the laws of Nature. The Christian, whose creed includes immortality as the birthright of his soul and the crown of his religious faith, resents the exclusion of all personal interest from the consideration of natural phenomena. For instance, with regard to the effect which physical death is supposed to exercise on his individuality, Science and Religion, regarding the phenomenon from different points of view, appear to be in opposition of opinion. But is this really the case? Is there not in reality fundamental unity between the secular and sacred aspects of all natural phenomena?

It has been suggested that the sliding scale of physical consciousness has its psychical counterpart in moral ideals, from which the aspirations and perceptions of men reach out towards spiritual apprehension. Can endorsement of this supposition be drawn from the realm of Natural Science? What reasonable evidence is forthcoming in support of the conjecture?

Although dogmatic distinction between the organic and inorganic kingdoms can be of no permanent value (since what is to-day classified as non-living matter may possibly to-morrow be declared to belong to the organic world), yet there is justification—drawn from observation of the simple characteristics of clearly defined organic and inorganic matter—for remarking the former to be distinguished by apparent sensory consciousness, which may therefore be called an active ingredient of manifested life; but the latter shows no such apparent consciousness, and can therefore be called a passive ingredient. Both forms of matter react upon each other, and are inextricably present in life contemplated as a whole. And both forms of matter are interdependent upon a logical sequence of action, by which the supreme Spirit of Life pervades and controls all manifested life. By this maintained interaction, perpetual manifestation of life is carried on, and the cycle of Birth and Death as a recurring demonstration of being is shown to be the transmuting accompaniment of the progressive will of the Spirit of Life. Continuance of sensation in an individual is dependent upon the maintenance of correspondence between its organisation and its environment, cessation of which is synonymous with death. In other words, matter hitherto possessing an individual consciousness, manifested by response to its environment, is resolved into particles of matter which show no united susceptibility to environment, and which are therefore not deserving of description as an individual living organism. Conversely, birth is a resolution of (in the above sense) inorganic matter into organic.

The more complicated an organism the wider its environment, and to the degree of its susceptibility the more liable to resolution into inorganic matter, unless a corresponding degree of ability to protect itself from danger continues to accompany its evolution. In the case of man, knowledge of how to maintain his bodily health must keep pace with intellectual development if the balance between physical consciousness and psychical apprehension is to be properly sustained. Psychical apprehension can be translated into physical comprehension only through the medium of sense, and appreciation of the meaning and value of spiritual life through the medium of the brain. Health of body is necessary for health of mind, and the co-operation of mind and body is necessary for the apprehension of spiritual truths.

Now consciousness, both in its physical and psychical aspects, is manifested by the response of an organism to its environment, and in the case of organisms characterised by the possession of brain, more particularly by the power to register sensation. Human consciousness is achieved largely by an ability to perceive and register *contrast* in the impressions conveyed to the understanding, and it is the exercising of this faculty which leads to an established recognition of Moral Law. Appreciation of the existence of shadow and darkness presupposes the existence of light, and distinction between these contrasts is summarised by the sense of sight. In like manner, the perception of truth rests upon the power to recognise falsehood, and an estimation of what constitutes honesty on a corresponding idea of dishonesty. The sensation of pleasure is obtained from the possession of a correspondingly acute capacity to feel pain, discrimination placing value on either polaric contrary proportionate to the sensory capacity involved. In short, the register of abstract qualities is more or less dependent upon an appreciation of their antitheses—the moral worth of virtue being determinable by the degree of perceptive discrimination displayed in recognition of its contrast. Just as vision is a result of light, only known to us as vision and formulated as such by reason of its contrast or absence, darkness, which spells blindness, so the idea of good is only known to us by force of its contrast, evil. Registration of the alternating sides of the swing of this polaric machinery of sense makes for an advance in moral and spiritual, as well as in physical consciousness. Evil, on the moral plane of consideration, is as entirely a result of ignorance and absence of good as blindness on the physical plane of actuality is the consequence of perpetual darkness, or insensibility to light. The negative elements of both conditions possess a potential possibility of transmutation into positive elements—the operation of psychical and physical alchemism forming the dual revelation of a God of Love, whereby those who are blind in spirit and body are made to see, to the end that the whole consciousness of man may be confirmed by his increasing knowledge of the glory of his Creator.

To be unable to suffer would entail insensibility to pleasure, and no moral meaning could in this case be evolved from and attached to the idea of feeling. But it is precisely by reason of his attainment of a high degree of consciousness, manifested by the ability to register sensation, that man can claim a comparatively high position in the evolutionary scale; and if suffering and death be indeed a result of his prehistoric interference with an originally painless scheme of Creation, it is difficult to reconcile the benefits he appears to have thereby gained with the idea of such being a punishment for his wrong-doing inflicted upon him by God. For since perception of contrast in abstract quality is absolutely necessary for the obtaining of conscience on the moral plane of thought—that is, for recognition of good and evil, and for the ability to transmute evil into good—it follows that where such perception does not exist there can be no moral responsibility attaching to individual action, no possibility of attaining a dominant spiritual consciousness, and no question of sharing the redemptive mission of Love. In the words of Christ, "If ye were blind, ye should have no sin: but now ye say, We see; therefore your sin remaineth" (St John ix. 41).

It is conceivable that just as that which to the eyes of men appears as darkness is not in the same degree dark to creatures whose habits have developed visual organs differing from those of man, so on the moral plane that which appears as evil to one man may to his differently developed brother seem less evil, and to creatures less highly organised than man, even good. No quality, physical, moral or spiritual, can be restricted or finally actualised; and no one man's opinion of what is estimable can stand as a perfectly true expression of any but his own ideas.

To sum up. The existence of pain is as necessary to the appreciation of pleasure as the existence of evil is to the appreciation of good. Therefore we may regard the sliding scale of consciousness as a register of sensation, a scale adapted to actual physical life and necessary for its continuity and development; and a scale which has its exact psychical counterpart in moral ideals, from which the evolving aspirations and perceptions of men reach out towards spiritual life. The degree of all quality, physical and moral, appears to be primarily dependent upon the capacity to feel—the capacity of consciousness. And upon the perception of contrast rests the possibility of attaining to a dominant plane of spiritual consciousness, and the power to become an active and willing agent in the divinely ordered transmuting, redemptive, and progressive government of life.

It is especially with regard to the spiritual consciousness of man, and of man's participation in the divine government of life, that the doctrine of Christ controverts the idea of suffering as an evil. In His verbal teaching, and in His rite of communion established as a symbolic epitome of His spiritual convictions, there is a clear acknowledgment of the fundamental unity of Nature—a basic point of argument which is also adopted to-day by every scientist in all departments of research. Christ laid particular emphasis upon the spiritual unity of man with God, He Himself speaking as a son of God—a manifestation of the divine Spirit of Life. He urged the following of His example upon His disciples, trying to open the blind eyes and deaf ears of men who had as yet so imperfect an understanding of spiritual things. He tried to teach them to look at life from His point of view. Did He not regard the son of man as the expression of God, recognition of which spiritual truth gave Him, as it can give to all, assurance of eternal life? The Spirit of Life which is in every man cannot die, for it is part of God, who is Life without beginning and without end.

Only the expression or medium of spirit, only the finite form, is mortal. Spirit is infinite and immortal.

Such sayings as the following, attributed to Christ and His disciples, are expressive of the relation of man to God, and each may be seen to form a logical corollary of the other:—

"I and my Father are one" (St John x. 30). This is the simple summary of Christ's conviction of fundamental union between the Spirit of Life, God, and manifested being.

"My Father is greater than I" (St John xiv. 28) expresses the fact that the Spirit of Life as a whole is greater than its manifested parts, although those parts are contained by the whole and are at one with the whole.

"He that hath seen me hath seen the Father" (St John xiv. 9). Here Christ speaks of Himself as a manifested part of the Spirit of Life, in which sense every man can see in his fellow-creatures the same manifested Spirit, who is God. He who looks at the son of man as the incarnate Son of God is following the example of Christ, who taught the brotherhood of man.

"No man hath seen God at any time" (St John i. 18)—shows the futility of imagining it possible to confine the supreme Spirit of Life in any one form at any one period of time. All form is manifested Spirit, but the Spirit of Life is not only in all, but over all.

The following, among very many other sayings, are also susceptible of the same interpretation:—

"I came from the Father, and am come into the world; again, I leave the world, and go to the Father" (St John xvi. 28).

"As the Father hath life in himself, so hath he given to the Son to have life in himself" (St John v. 26).

This doctrine of Christ, indicative of His sense of union between God as the supreme Spirit of Life and of individual being—a union unbroken by the incidents of birth and death attendant upon the manifestation of the Spirit—harmonises with the scientific doctrine of the unity of nature, and if accepted as a fundamental clue to His reported words and deeds, very many of the difficulties and supposed inconsistencies apparent in a purely ecclesiastical interpretation of His person and mission melt away, leaving a beautiful coherency of religious truth in accord with the revelations of natural science.

When men look at life from Christ's point of view, thereby attaining recognition of God as their Father, they become spiritual creatures who hold the moral responsibility of their beings in trust to the Spirit of Life. Christ lived in advance of the intellectual thought of His day, having intuitive knowledge of the unity of nature, but no scientific evidence to offer in its support. But His life and doctrine afford convincing illustrations of His spiritual convictions, and the key to the mystery of His miraculous works of love may perhaps be found in our realisation of His sense of kinship with all living creatures. His acquiescence with natural laws, known by Him to be the working of the will of the Spirit of Life, gave Him influence over all persons with whom He was able to establish a spiritual relation—with all who were willing to co-operate with Him in the alchemistic law of love. His own self-command gave Him dominion over those weaker than Himself, who did not resist His will, who, in the language of Scripture, "had faith in Him." Without such faith we are told He could do no mighty works. But given this receptive attitude of mind, He was able to infuse strength into a sick person and thus to stimulate the Spirit to resume its normal correspondence with the functions of the flesh.

Realisation of union with God as the supreme Spirit of Life entails an awakening to the significance of the unity of nature, and calls for an adjustment of the physical equipment of sense into accord with what is perceived to be the will of the Spirit of Life. With the desire to be at one with the Will of God, consciousness of those influences hitherto dimly apprehended to control existence as though by autocratic law, widens into perception of a progressive government of the whole of life, in the ordinance of which men may take an active part. Here, surely, is that recognition of God possible to all, to which Christ referred in the words, "God is a Spirit, and they that worship him must worship him in spirit and in truth" (St John iv). This is that heaven of light and truth, to be excluded from which is to dwell in the outer darkness of spiritual ignorance. And this is the new birth unto righteousness with a death unto sin which is the epitome of the ethical teaching of Christ.

But, it will be asked, how does this view of life eliminate suffering as an evil from the world? How can it be shown that disease and death, the fear and danger of which cast a perpetual shadow over life, are not evil things, responsible as such for the suffering of all creatures? Granted that man has attained his present high position in the evolutionary scale chiefly through his ability to feel, to suffer; granted that the establishment of morality, brought about largely by registration of contrast in sensation, leads directly to realisation of spiritual life; granted that we may be privileged thereby to exercise a transmuting influence upon evil and its effects, thus making us partakers in the progressive government of life; if our future evolution, proceeding on the same lines of development, entails an ever greater capacity to suffer, is it a desirable thing? Have not less highly organised creatures, with correspondingly lower degrees of consciousness and with less knowledge of the governing principle of life and their own responsibility towards that government, happier lives than men? Whither are we tending? What is the ultimate goal of the recurring cycle of birth and death, manifested by the operation of natural laws, in the general scheme of life in which the evolution of man is but a part?

The welfare of individual man has no meaning apart from its relation to the benefit of mankind as a progressive whole. If a man participate in the common habits of his fellows, he must take his share in those dangers to individual existence which the development of his race necessitates. The advantages which we to-day derive from our employment of social and scientific contrivances common to civilised communities have been wrought from the effort and suffering of men of past times. We are debtors to our ancestors who, by their own labour and sacrifice, have given us a better equipment for the battle of life than was their own inheritance from their forefathers. We are under an obligation to our race which, whether we discharge it willingly or no, is drawn from us by the operation of forces beyond our own control, as the just equivalent of our gain. We cannot separate ourselves, humanly speaking, from our kind. Inasmuch as the spirit of humanity reaches out towards immortality from one generation to another, our lives are not our own. Rather are they hostages to fortune, to that evolutionary principle which, while allowing us as individuals to participate in the benefits actualised to-day as the results of the labours of past generations of men, also exacts from us our own contribution towards the slow perfecting of our kind.

It is indubitable that suffering is an important factor in the evolution of the mind as well as of the body of man. Inefficiency and defect in scientific and social contrivances are made apparent by accident, which, having entailed human suffering, is therefore productive of effort to rectify the cause of danger, and thus of reducing the risk of further punishment.

Could perfect correspondence between an organism and its environment be perpetually maintained, physical death could only occur as the final stage in the gradual decline of the medium of the spirit. Such natural dissolution appears to be part of the order of manifested life, requisite for its continuity and for the evolution of species, and necessary for the development of the spiritual desire for immortality. It is not of necessity a painful process, since the slow decline in physical vitality implies a corresponding decrease in sensibility, or, in other words, a decrease of physical consciousness. Premature death, the result of disease and accident, and accompanied by more or less suffering, constitutes the wages of ignorance, and only in this sense can pain and death be said to be a punishment for sin inflicted by God. If man, individually and socially, does not know how to protect himself from danger, he must pay the penalty for ignorance. Only a perfected organism, maintaining a permanent correspondence with its environment, could be permanently capable of combating physical death. And since the cycle of the birth and death of all forms of life constitutes the central principle of natural law, it is difficult to imagine an eventual eternal preservation of individual physical life to be the ordained end of the evolution of humanity.

When life is looked at as a whole—a point of view entailing perception of God as the supreme Spirit of Life informing and governing all matter—there appears no injustice in the suffering of the human race, or of other organisms whose evolution requires their conscious susceptibility to environment. Men must suffer for their ignorance in order to become wise, and to get wisdom they must eat from the tree of good and evil. Those who are ignorant of what is necessary for the preservation of health receive the wages of their imperfection—suffering, and premature death unto the third and fourth generations—not as the vindictive vengeance of an offended

Deity, but as the remedial vindication of a persisting will of love, a transmuting process which must endure until the result of fatal ignorance is expurgated from a progressive world.

If individual thought, individual free-will and action, were more generally recognised to be the prime factors by which human evolution is forwarded or deterred; if concern for the preservation of individual advantage were dominated by a desire to promote the welfare of the race; if the willing transmutation by vicarious suffering of the effects of evil into elements of good were more readily accepted as the privilege of the members of the communion of love; we are justified in believing that unnatural suffering and death, with their manifold accompaniment of sorrow and fear, would be gradually eliminated from the lives of men according as they grew into a more perfect wisdom and understanding of the meaning and purpose of life.

Like Christ, we must be perfected through suffering. The whole creation groaneth and travaileth together, to the end that the incarnate purpose of life may be fulfilled, and that the increasing sum of the spiritual consciousness of creation may be brought into co-operation with the Divine Creator and so actively and willingly share in the divine government of life.

V

THE VESTURE OF GOD

When Paul of Tarsus reproved the men of Athens for ignorantly worshipping an unknown God, he was virtually denouncing the tendency towards idolatry which is inherent in all religious symbolism. Public worship of an unknown and unseen God must be more or less symbolic in order to express any particular idea of the nature of the supposed divinity. But a stranger in a strange land, uninitiated into the symbolism of the religious faith there practised, is apt to infer idolatry in the ritual he witnesses simply because he cannot discriminate between the thing seen and its esoteric significance. The programme of Christianity delivered by St Paul to the Athenians practically excluded ceremony as a necessary accompaniment of worship. He preached a known God, a seen God, revealed in the person of Jesus Christ, and requiring no likening unto gold, silver, or stone images, graven by art and men's devices.

It is noteworthy that every religion in its infancy is but sparely attended by forms and ceremonies, the more or less elaborate ritual that accompanies its subsequent growth being an almost inevitable result of its consolidation into a definite creed which shall stand as the supposed likeness of its original spiritual conception. This rise of ritual is largely responsible for the need of periodical reform which is a common occurrence in the development of every religion that has outlived its infancy. The history of Christianity, with which alone we have here to deal, affords recurring examples of agitation directed against a perverted religious symbolism—a dangerous degeneration which, by crushing the spirit beneath the letter of observance, leads to hypocritical and idolatrous practices.

It is difficult to think that St Paul, when condemning the symbolic worship of the Athenians and Ephesians, foresaw the growth of that elaborate ritual, formulated gradually as symbolic evidence of Christian doctrine, which has become so inextricably a part of the Catholic faith as taught in the Church to-day. Christ's remark, "Except ye be converted, and become as little children, ye shall not enter into the kingdom of heaven" (Matt. xviii. 3), might with advantage be applied to religious organisations as well as to individuals. But although as a reformer of the Jewish faith He denounced symbolism, which had become corrupt, inasmuch as undue stress was laid upon the letter to the neglect of the spirit of the law, He yet submitted to the ordinance of the law in all particulars, perceiving that a proper attention to the spirit did not necessarily entail neglect of the letter of its observance. He was a reformer, not an iconoclast. He came not to destroy, but to fulfil. But His outspoken denunciation of the hypocritical and idolatrous practices of the Scribes and Pharisees roused an active hostility to His teaching, since reversion to the simple ethical principles such as was advocated by the later prophets, with a proper appreciation of symbolism as symbolism, implied the downfall of those whose tenure of authority over the masses of the people depended upon the strict maintenance of a complicated and mystifying ritual.

Symbolic worship is an attestation to an unseen God, its ostensible purpose being of course that a gradual revelation of God may be vouchsafed to the pious devotees of sacraments and ceremonies. The inaugurator of a rite, desiring to express his ideas of abstract or absolute truth, contrives a symbol, a work of art that shall stand as the likeness of his thoughts—a likeness capable of carrying significance according to the discriminating intelligence of all who may behold it. He cannot be held responsible for any subsequent confounding of his artistic symbol with its esoteric meaning; but to those who cannot distinguish between an image and its significance—who interpret the letter as synonymous with the spirit of a rite—the observance of symbolic worship becomes perforce an introductory step towards idolatry, the practice of which is fatal to intellectual and spiritual progress.

Not only with regard to religion, but in every branch of art, in the common habits of daily life, in the very language that clothes thought, this dangerous tendency of the human mind towards idolatry may be observed. Thus, worship of beauty for beauty's sake is idolatrous. But its recognition as the outward sign of inner grace is one of the lay sacraments of life which link the real to the ideal realm of thought and give an added glory to human existence. Is not man a dual creature? Is not his body an artistic expression of the divine Spirit of Life, in whose likeness he is made? And are not his works representations of his creative and executive powers, even as the works of nature are representations of the supreme Spirit of Life?

The minds of individuals, as of races, find expression in their works, the worth of all artistic symbols of endeavour (whether of so-called secular or sacred significance) being determined by the evidential testimony they convey of abstract and absolute truth. Now, illumination of unproven supposition being prefatory to its establishment as fact, the evidence of things unseen and unknown is resolved into the foundation of comprehension. The execution of a work of art is only truly estimable when its realism affords an adequate expression of its maker's mind—when, in short, it forms the outward sign of inward meaning, and is recognisable as such.

Thus considered, words stand as symbols, language being evidence of thought. The extent of a man's vocabulary may be taken as a fair criterion of his ideas about the things of which his words are the expression, always supposing he does not fall into idolatrous worship of words as words, to the neglect of their proper significance and value. Again, figures as symbols of calculative thought, while valueless in themselves, are of inestimable importance when rightly utilised as an effective means to an end. Through the science of mathematics, the relation between magnitudes only conceivable to the mathematician by his employment of calculative symbols, can be correctly ascertained, and a working hypothesis for practical purposes thereby obtained. Mathematical formulæ thus regarded appear as the outer signs of a reasoning process that resolves the unseen and unknown into proven facts.

The rituals of religious creeds, regarded as combinations of symbols as infinite in variety and arrangement as the needs of men, may surely be designated as works of art if it be remembered that admiration and imitation of natural objects is mainly responsible for the conception of those several deities whose supposed supernatural authority forms the summit of each particular creed, and whose character stands not only as a summary of a people's appreciation of what is admirable in human conduct, but also as an expression of artistic feeling.

Growth of art is proportionate to intellectual development. That is to say, expression follows conception—a precept evidenced by the progressive works of men, which bear witness to their makers' increasing power to give utterance to what has hitherto been unutterable because incomprehensible. Thus considered, symbolism appears as the *alphabet of truth*, whereby men may read the history of past days, and write the record of their own achievements in the Book of Time. It is the link between seen and unseen, real and ideal, knowledge and mystery, finite and infinite. It is the seal of divinity set upon man who, made in the image of God—an artistic expression of the supreme Spirit of Life—is endowed with the attributes of his Creator, thereby enabled to manifest his creative energy in his own works of art and so to offer continual testimony to the indwelling and divine Spirit of his life. Thus the glory of the Creator is made visible to His creatures not only in the wonders of the natural world scientifically revealed in the course of intellectual development, but also in a correspondingly progressive spiritual revelation of essential truth behind the vesture of symbolic being.

Contemplative life is to men the reflection of their minds, Nature acting as the mirror of those mental visions which connect thought with spiritual perception. And since psychical ideals are regulated by intellectual limitations, *understanding* of spiritual truths must be proportionate to intellectual insight.

Jesus Christ offered no evidence of the essential truth of His spiritual convictions save by symbolism. Like all idealists, He sought by means of art to convey His ideas to the understanding of His disciples. This was done in three ways. He spoke in parables; His actions were dramatically contrived to illustrate His verbal teaching; and He ordained a ceremony, the performance of which should perpetuate the epitome of His doctrine. His view of life being the reflection of His spiritual ideals, and more or less dependent upon His intellectual perceptions, it was necessary, in order to make others see as He saw, to teach them to look at life from His point of view.

He saw the earth and the fulness thereof as the outer sign of the supreme Spirit of Life—Nature being the vesture of God, the cloak of spirit, making all creatures likenesses of God and manifestations of the divine will. God's works of art—natural phenomena—are variously interpreted, because men's spiritual perception is regulated by their intellectual capacity to understand what they perceive. In the same way the symbolic works of art employed by Christ to illustrate His teaching are variously interpreted according to men's ability to grasp the true inner meaning behind the vesture of parable and ritual. His symbolic teaching was interpreted literally by the materialists among His audiences. Only a few understood that He spoke in parables, and that His actions were intended to illustrate spiritual truths. Even His chosen disciples failed sometimes to distinguish between the outer signs of His doctrine and their inner significance. But Christ looked to the future for a wider acceptance of His gospel of love and its application to the whole scheme of life. He foresaw that by the spirit of truth inherent in all knowledge and emanating from the supreme Spirit of Life, His teaching would be tested and purged of whatever false interpretations idolatrous generations of men might place upon it. "Heaven and earth shall pass away, but my words shall not pass away" (Matt. xxi. 35). Truth is not bounded by the duration of men's finite term of earthly life.

For the sake, therefore, of unborn generations of men He desired to safeguard the perpetuation of His ideas of truth, so that they might carry their message to a future and more spiritually minded age. Would not a comprehensive symbol, a rite, carrying significance proportionate to the discriminating intelligence of those who should witness it, combat the danger of His doctrine becoming irretrievably corrupted? The foundation of His gospel of love lay in His sense of union between God as the supreme Spirit of Life and individual being—every form of life appearing to Him as a manifestation of God and a part of the Divine essence. The symbol He contrived must be closely associated with Himself and with this doctrine. It must be the likeness of His idea, and as a true work of art it must be capable of conveying its meaning to all able to recognise a spiritual truth beneath its outward form. It must be the epitome of all that was of vital importance in

His teaching. It must be suited to all countries, and to all manner of men at all times. And in order to ensure its faithful perpetuation, it must be inaugurated as a personal memorial of Himself, to be celebrated through all ages as a symbol of the spiritual unity of life. What more fitting material for His purpose than the common daily food and drink of people of all classes? What could better illustrate the bond of union existing throughout Nature than a ceremony which should show how living creatures are sustained by the fruits of the earth, and which should emphasise the fact that animate and inanimate Nature is pervaded by the same Spirit of Life which works through a recurring cycle of birth and death for a perpetual manifestation of God, *who is Life*, the vital principle of being? What could better illustrate this Spirit of Life dwelling in men's bodies and making them temples of God than a rite which drew attention to the fact that nourishment of the body is necessary for the continuance of the manifestation of the Spirit? Bread, the staff of life, is in some form or other the daily food of all peoples. The tilling of the fields, the garnering of the grain, the grinding of the corn, bring men into intimate relation with Nature, and fittingly demonstrate that connection between natural laws and the lives of men fundamental to their existence and necessary for the maintenance of life. The vine served as the subject of some of Christ's most beautiful parables; it was an object of familiar interest to the people of Judæa; its cultivation was associated with the habits of their daily lives. Its fruit was thus another suitable symbol of intercommunion between the products of the earth and the bodies of men.

The accounts of the inauguration of the rite of communion given by St Matthew, St Mark, and St Luke agree in the statement that it occurred when Christ and His disciples met together to celebrate the Feast of the Passover, immediately before the betrayal by Judas. The occasion was clearly chosen by Christ as suitable in all respects for the institution of the ceremony He had conceived as adequately embodying a symbolic epitome of His doctrine. Throughout His mission He had rigorously observed the letter of the Jewish law, it being in accord with His office as a reformer of a distorted religious symbolism to utilise existing ritual in order to expatiate on its neglected spiritual significance. The keeping of the Passover with His twelve disciples could be made to signify very much. It would be the last Passover He would keep with them. Nay, more, it would be the last meal.

When the Feast next occurred this present celebration would be remembered as the last occasion when He had broken bread with them. All that He had then said and done would be graven on their memories as the last words and deeds of their beloved Master before He was taken from them to undergo His trial and death. He would appeal, therefore, to their affectionate memory of Him in order to induce a faithful performance of the rite He was inaugurating. Though they might fail to grasp its full spiritual significance, their attachment to Him would ensure the carrying out of His command to fulfil it in memory of Him. If the faithful celebration of the rite were secured, there was made possible a fuller understanding of its meaning by future and more enlightened generations, who would subject His doctrine to the test of the Spirit of Truth, proceeding from the supreme Spirit of Life, and inherent in all knowledge.

St John gives no account of the institution of the rite at the time of the Passover, although he alone of the four Evangelists reports Christ's verbal teaching of the doctrine thus embodied on occasions other than its inauguration as a symbol of communion. In the sixth chapter of his gospel we find Christ reported as using the same symbolic phraseology with regard to His flesh and blood that He employed in His speech introducing the rite at the Last Supper. We read of the disciples and the Jews disputing Christ's words, interpreting them literally, and calling forth His explanation that "It is the Spirit that quickeneth; the words that I speak unto you, they are spirit and they are life." Notwithstanding the implied injunction that His doctrine of the unity of life was to be interpreted in a spiritual sense, we find that "from that time many of his disciples went back, and walked no more with him."

Since then, how many literal interpreters of Christ's symbolic utterances have turned aside from following after Him, and have been led away into idolatrous worship of the letter of His teaching to the neglect of its spiritual significance!

It would appear that the symbolic epitome of the doctrine of communion had been conceived by Christ some time before He introduced it as a rite on the occasion of the Last Supper; that the idea had already been verbally expounded by Him; and that its consolidation into the form eventually chosen was achieved as a dramatic finale to the whole of His previous teaching. If the fourth gospel be the work of John, the disciple whom Christ loved, it is significant that he alone reported the injunction that Christ's words were to be interpreted in a spiritual sense. The doctrine of the unity of life, incorporated in the rite of communion, permeates the whole of the gospel, and lends strength to the supposition that its writer had in some special way known personal intimacy with Christ. Union between God as the supreme Spirit of Life, and the Word as the expression of God, is the basis of its doctrinal construction; and the institution of the rite of communion, duly reported in the other gospels, is here shown to be the logical conclusion, in the form of a symbolic epitome, of the premisses adopted by the writer.

Supposition, however, is not evidence. In order to determine the significance of the rite of communion, and thus to arrive at some idea of its importance in Christian doctrine, it is necessary to subject it to that test which Christ Himself declared to be the proper criterion of merit—the Spirit of Truth. In these later days, nearly two thousand years since He utilised the loving obedience of His disciples to institute symbolic evidence of the spiritual unity of life—a rite designed to give light to untold generations to come—how have men obeyed His injunction to test His words and deeds by the Spirit of Truth?

"The Comforter, which is the Holy Ghost, whom the Father will send in my name, he shall teach you all things, and bring all things to your remembrance, whatsoever I have said unto you" (St John xiv. 26).

"When the Comforter is come, whom I will send unto you from the Father, even the Spirit of truth which proceedeth from the Father, he shall testify of me" (St John xv. 26).

"I have yet many things to say unto you, but ye cannot bear them now. Howbeit when he, the Spirit of truth, is come, he will guide you into all truth: for he shall not speak of himself; but whatsoever he shall hear, that shall he speak: and he will show you things to come. He shall glorify me; for he shall receive of mine, and shall show it unto you" (St John xvi. 12).

In these sayings, among very many others, we have a declaration that the Spirit of Truth, inherent in knowledge and proceeding from God, the supreme Spirit of Life, accompanies intellectual and spiritual evolution.

Christ's doctrine was not intended only for His immediate followers and men of His own race and time. Much that was to them incomprehensible, much that by reason of their intellectual limitations He could only teach by implication, He referred to future generations of men who might discover and appreciate by the clearer light of after-days the intrinsic truth of His doctrine of spiritual unity. How has His appeal to posterity been answered? How has His recommendation to test His words by the Spirit of Truth been obeyed?

It is part of the function of scientific criticism to examine emotional apprehension, and to corroborate or disprove by means of evidential testimony the truth in spiritual suppositions. The modern view of the universe, which recognises for the elements of matter an essential correlation of principle, may thus be regarded as the rational endorsement of Christ's spiritual apprehension of the intercommunion and oneness of all forms of life. That the bodies of men are reared upon and sustained by innumerable other forms of life; that every individual is in reality an aggregate of others; that Nature rests upon the continued intercommunion of all its parts; that no one part has power and meaning save in conjunction with others; that correlation is the perpetuating principle of life; that the very universe depends upon the mutual support of its component parts—are scientific facts that have their psychical counterparts in the spiritual ideals contained in Christ's gospel of love, and are emphasised in the symbolic summary of His teaching—the rite of communion.

Let us now take the actual words supposed to have been used on the occasion of the inauguration of this rite, and examine them by the light of attested scientific facts:—

"Take eat, this is my body which is given for you."

"This cup is the New Testament of my blood which is shed for you."

Christ spoke as an incarnate son of God, as a human manifestation of the Spirit of Life. His form, derived from and nourished by the fruits of the earth, was in its elemental essence one with the vital principle of all forms of life. The bread was His body. His physical life was sustained by His participation in the sacrificial intercommunion of Nature. But the time was come when His body was to suffer death. He had risked His life by preaching reformatory doctrine. Now this work was done. He was aware of His impending death, therefore He would not eat again. But His disciples were not yet to die, for their work was not yet done. Therefore He bid them eat and drink, and thus continue to benefit from the intercommunion of Nature, in which all forms of life obtain mutual sustenance by mutual sacrifice.

The wine was His blood. In an agricultural and vine-growing country such as Judæa, bread and wine were suitable examples of nutriment necessary for the maintenance of physical life. The flesh and blood of men are drawn from the products of the earth, and are resolved into their elemental parts when the spirit is separated by death from the body. Starvation weakens and finally destroys the body, but nourishment restores waste and makes continued manifestation of the spirit possible. Christ's blood had been formed from the fruits of the earth. Now it was to be shed. Sacrifice according to the Jewish law necessitated the shedding of blood. Was not the Feast of the Passover, which He was then keeping with His apostles, a sacrifice of blood? But He announced the institution of a new testimony of His blood which should not only witness to His death, but should show forth the victory of the Spirit over physical dissolution. The symbol of sacrifice was to be spiritualised. Whereas the old Jewish idea of worship necessitated the taking of life and emphasised the shedding of blood as pleasing to God, the spiritual significance of sacrifice was now re-illustrated by Christ's new interpretation of the sacrament of life. The kindly fruits of the earth; the increase of the earth; the bursting forth of vital energy from the earth—was now to yield the symbolism of the communion of life. Not death, but life was to be emphasised as the will of God. The veil of the Spirit was to be lifted, showing Nature as the outer sign of life, as the veritable vesture of God.

It is noteworthy that this interpretation of the rite of communion in no way contradicts the constructions placed upon it by the Catholic Church. Instead, it reconciles certain differences of opinion, and may be seen to offer a point where religion and science may meet in a special endorsement of the unity of Nature.

The doctrine of transubstantiation is coherent and reasonable if prefaced by recognition of God as the supreme Spirit of Life present in all form. It is absence of this spiritual acknowledgment that has laid the teaching of the Church of Rome open to the charge of idolatry. Both before and after the "consecration," the bread and wine are most truly the body and blood of God if Nature be recognised as the vesture of the Divine Spirit. The repetition of the words spoken by Christ at His institution of the rite serve to emphasise this spiritual truth. The idea of *corporal* union with Christ, obtained by partaking of the consecrated elements, does not adequately illustrate the fact that all life is one, and that all form is pervaded by the same one Spirit of Life. His body and blood is not the only touch-stone of union among men, since the whole of Nature is one communion of life, wherein all creatures are one by reason of their common spiritual source of life. The same principle by which the fruits of the earth built up and sustained the human body of Christ works to-day throughout Nature. Here, indeed, is the outer sign of the sacrament of union, as illustrated in His rite of communion. But the spiritual significance of this kinship of Nature there made evident, although latent in the Roman interpretation of the rite, suffers neglect in practice, and its symbolism is thus in danger of degeneration towards idolatry.

The English version inclines towards the other extreme by unduly neglecting the outer sign of union, thus detracting from the full significance of the rite. It does not emphasise the corporate brotherhood of man, and it does not therefore appear fully in accord with the scientific doctrine of the unity of Nature. In striving to avoid the supposed idolatrous errors of Rome, the rite has been deprived of half its meaning. The Church of England strains towards a spiritual interpretation at the expense of the actual; whereas the Church of Rome accentuates the actual to the neglect of the spiritual. Neither version attains an adequate appreciation of the fact that the rite of communion is primarily a symbol, whose meaning can only be properly gauged by due attention to both its outward sign and its inner meaning. The spiritual is manifested through the actual, as the infinite through the finite. Understanding of essential truth is gained through the senses, not in spite of them. But the word is neither of greater or lesser importance than the thought. Is not the one an expression of the other, as Nature—the vesture of God—is the expression of the Spirit of Life? Thus, in the words of Christ: "I have manifested thy name unto the men which thou gavest me out of the world: I have given them thy word. Thy word is truth" (St John xvii.).

If God be recognised as the supreme Spirit of Life, love must be seen to be the expression of life, and the perpetuating principle of life. Life is a whole, and the Spirit of Life pervading all form is manifested by the intercommunion of all its parts. Thus, the formation of flower and fruit secure the perpetuation of plant life, with whose existence is entwined the preservation of other forms of life. With higher organisms propagation is achieved by the same principle of sacrificial love, the intercommunion of all forms of life being necessary for the continuity of life as a whole.

Thus considered, love appears as a symbol, the outer sign of the sacrament of life, wherein individuals are united in spirit, and as a consequence of this union obtain increasing consciousness of their immortality. The attainment of such spiritual consciousness entails the subservience of personal identity to the consciousness of kinship with the Whole of Life. Christ's gospel of love, with its repeated assertions of the necessity for self-surrender as prefatory to the acquirement of spiritual joy, finds a parallel in the pursuit of happiness undertaken by men and women in the occurrences of everyday life. Do not the joys of love in its human relations between friends, husband and wife, parents and children, rest on a mutual surrender of self-interest?

The rite of communion can thus be resolved into a sacramental work of art, whose outer sign is love, and whose inner meaning is life. Through Christ's symbolic work of art, the vesture of God which manifests the Spirit of Life is seen to rest upon all form. The symbols chosen by Him to summarise His teaching are of an exact appropriateness. By His illustrations of bread and wine, designated by Him as His flesh and blood, the gospel of love and the scientific doctrine of the common derivative union of all forms of life are brought together and shown to be the inseparable accompaniment of the whole of manifested life. Therefore the declaration, "This is my body.... This is my blood ..." is not only true of the physical relationship which He Himself bore to Nature as the vesture of the Spirit of Life, but is applicable in its verity to every man who, in obedience to Christ's command to "Do this in remembrance of me," comes to recognise in his employment of the prescribed formula the true expression of his own union with the elements of Nature, and his own relation to the supreme Spirit of Life as a child of God, made manifest through love.

Christ's words are not therefore to be repeated only as a quotation of a formula applicable solely to Himself as a being differing from all other men, by reason of a divine origin possessed by Him alone; but as living truth, capable of realisation by every thinking man and woman as an epitomised testimony to the essential unity of all forms of life, a unity manifested in form by the perpetuating principle of love.

This unity of Nature is attested by the intercommunion maintained between its parts through the mutual surrender of individual advantage and personal identity, which sacrifice enables the perpetuation of the whole of manifested life to be carried on.

"For whosoever will save his life shall lose it: but whosoever will lose his life for my sake, the same shall save it" (St Luke ix. 24).

In these words Christ, conscious of Himself as a manifestation of the supreme Spirit of Life, and speaking as Incarnate Love, urges a similar spiritual realisation on His fellow-men; so that they also, through voluntary self-surrender in the communion of love, may obtain spiritual union with the Source of Life, and become consciously clothed with the vesture of God.

VI

SPIRITUAL CORRESPONDENCE

CAREFUL examination of the articles of most religious creeds reveals so remarkable a connection between the ideas of prayer and immortality inculcated therein, that in an attempt to trace and summarise the effect of either of these devotional outcomes of the religious sense over the spiritual evolution of mankind, it is expedient to subject them to a dual consideration.

The infinite diversity of the human mind is made strikingly apparent by the different ideas of the significance and utility of prayer existing at various periods in the history of religion; and if this exercise of the evolving soul of man be recognised as yielding the basis of those conceptions of human immortality which, when defined as the goal of established creeds, distinguish such from all purely philosophical systems of thought, the difficulty of dissociating these two devotional factors in the development of spiritual correspondence becomes even more clearly apparent.

It is noteworthy that most interpretations of the function of prayer, although acknowledging its fundamental purpose to be that of providing a means of direct communication between God and man, vary according to the different conceptions of the nature of God of which prayer is the logical corollary, and from which all ideas of immortality are derived. For instance, the notion of God as a Person, made in the image of man, and endowed with his characteristics and powers in a superlatively human degree, is naturally accompanied by belief in the efficacy of prayer as a means of modifying the circumstances of life by permitting them to deviate from the normal operating sequence of cause and effect, into irregular acquiescence with the particular and changing desires of individuals. Such an interpretation of the use of prayer is chiefly characteristic of the religious history of the childhood of the human race; but it also represents a type of mind surviving to-day under the domination of ecclesiastical Christianity which, inculcating the theory that the government of God in the world is directed towards the especial benefit of mankind at the expense of the so-called "lower creation," is largely responsible for those ideas of inconsistency between the principles of religion and science which have led to controversial warfare between these two educative influences of the human mind.

Most of the conceptions of immortality which accompany belief in a purely personal Deity trend towards an actual epitomised realisation of all that appears possible to obtain from God through the medium of prayer. The savage, attributing to his deity the power of capriciously inflicting upon him pain and pleasure, misery and happiness, prays for the satisfaction of his personal desires, and for immunity and protection from bodily harm. His ideas of immortality hover consequently about the imagined summarised reality of his prayers—Heaven being conceived of as a place where the human joys for which he has prayed can be realised in a magnified degree for ever; and Hell as the threatened compendium of all his fears, the culmination of pains and perils, to escape which he offers up propitiatory and supplicating prayer.

In order to guard as far as possible against verbal misunderstanding, it is perhaps as well to offer a definition of the sense in which the word prayer is here used.

The expression of the desire to correspond with the will of God.

Have we not here a basic point of spiritual correspondence, from which man's hope of immortality may be seen to justify its conception?

Careful consideration of the many and apparently conflicting methods of enunciating prayer leads to the observation that there exist practically but two great categories into which all varieties of prayer naturally fall:—

1. "Prayer of Specific Petition"—the outcome of the physical susceptibilities of men.

2. "Prayer of Spiritual Acquiescence"—the expression of the psychical apprehensions of men working through the medium of sense into perception of God as the supreme Spirit of Life, revealed in form, and present as the Spirit of Truth in knowledge.

The one is antecedent to the other. That is to say, prayer of spiritual acquiescence is a natural growth from prayer of specific petition, observation of which fact offers striking evidence of the evolution of the soul of man.

It is one of the foremost characteristics of youth to demand from established authority satisfaction of those mental and physical desires which growth of consciousness entails. A child naturally attributes to his parents the ability to grant or to deny his requests. He receives from them all the necessaries of life; reward and punishment are in their keeping; and he therefore conceives the idea of propitiating their good-will towards him, trying by his conduct to rouse the approval and pleasure and avert the wrath of the parental government. He is disappointed when his requests are refused or ignored, and grateful when they are granted, perceiving himself at the mercy of a strength and power greater than his own.

Under precisely the same circumstances of ignorant youth, the so-called "uncivilised man" bows to the authority of what he believes to be supernatural power exerted upon him by the gods. He is, apparently, the plaything of a capricious deity, who holds as clay within his hands those conditions of life which bind him to his fate. Surely he does wisely to propitiate this authoritative power by gifts, vows, and supplications; by thank-offerings for danger averted; by petitions for the deliverance from threatened evil. Before all serious undertakings he tries by means of omens to read the will of his god towards him, even as the little children, studying their parents' faces, hope to discern thereon the propitious moment for the voicing of a particular request. But there comes a time when the child ceases to be a child; when he puts aside childish things—idle questions and unreasoning entreaties; when he no longer asks in words for the satisfaction of each transitory desire; when he acquiesces with perfect confidence in that loving wisdom of his father, which experience has proved to him to be a will for his own good in conjunction with the good of the whole of life; when the reasonableness of such acquiescence with his father's will controls his thoughts and pervades his consciousness; when the maturing man, looking out with awakened perceptions of the order of the world, recognises the will of God, written upon the face of Nature, as the true revelation of his own will. His mode of prayer has changed. Spiritual acquiescence has taken the place of specific petition. He enters into fuller understanding of the works of his Father; he approaches communion of consciousness with the supreme Spirit of Life.

Development of the desire to correspond with the will of God accompanies both the spiritual progress of the individual consciousness of men and of the collective consciousness of mankind. That is to say, the evolution of prayer here suggested—showing how a faithful desire to know and to do the will of God induces its own fulfilment by growing consciousness of and acquiescence with the divine Spirit of Life—is not only applicable to individual effort, but also to those combinations of aspiration which we designate as public prayer. For if the repetition of a sincere desire to be, say, moral, be in an individual a strong bias towards morality, the office of general prayer, employed for a like congregational purpose, must be capable of carrying with its rehearsal a similar inducement towards its own fulfilment.

But although a priest may give utterance to the noblest of sentiments, to the highest and purest aspirations of those human hearts whose mouth-piece he professedly is, if the spirit of sincere individual desire be not instilled into the spoken prayer that is supposed to represent the congregational will, performance of the office becomes a mockery of its intention, its expression as surely falling into nothingness as the echoes of the human voice fade to silence. But when the performance of public prayer is truly utilised to express the united wills of many individuals, such a concentration of desire must make for fulfilment by means as purely natural as those by which the laws of demand and supply operate in life—the medium between desire and its fulfilment being the operating power of will. If the efficacy of public prayer were more generally recognised, surely there might be added to orthodox liturgies an increasing power which would illuminate the idea of the divinity of man, witness to the glory of the government of God, and bring into a union of love the souls of the children of God. For word is the fruit of the Spirit which brings into being the germ of the deed that shall, at the appointed time, fulfil the purpose of its being.

To those thinkers whose spiritual perceptions have been quickened by the doctrine of the unity of Nature into recognition of God as the Spirit of Life present in all form, a connection between prayer and immortality will be plainly evident. But if the idea of the aim of prayer which accompanies the interpretation of Nature as the vesture of God be that of voluntary effort to become one with the Divine Will, what idea of immortality is the natural outcome of such belief?

If we assume Christ's conception of God to have been drawn from His interpretation of Nature as the vesture of the Divine Spirit of Life, we may expect to find some presage of His ideas relating to the immortality of man in His teaching concerning the meaning and function of prayer.

The so-called "Lord's Prayer" is commonly accepted as summarising His doctrine relating to the right rendering of prayer, and offers a remarkable illustration of that combined specific petition and spiritual acquiescence which is characteristic of His own employment of prayer.

In His dual capacity of reformer of a corrupted religious symbolism and innovator of new esoteric ideas, He sought to cultivate a new order from the old, not by grafting upon past habit and tradition the bud of an extraneous growth, but by inviting the co-operation of the free-will of men with the working of the natural laws of development, perceived by Him to offer a means of attaining to a higher plane of spiritual consciousness. When He told His disciples that "All things whatsoever ye shall ask in prayer, believing, ye shall receive," He tacitly acknowledged the value of specific petitionary prayer, the right employment of which we know to be capable of providing an educational basis for the attaining of higher ideas of the relation between things material and things spiritual.

But His advocacy of all such specific petition was accompanied by a prefatory acknowledgment of God as the Father of man, the natural expression of His sense of union with the supreme Spirit and Source of Life. On the occasion of His own prayer before His betrayal, we find an expression both of His physical and spiritual desires. The man prays that suffering may be averted from him, while the spirit voices its longing to conform to God's Will and thus to obtain perfect union with the Spirit of Life in him and over him.

"Abba, Father, all things are possible unto thee; take away this cup from me: nevertheless not what I will, but what thou wilt" (St Mark xiv. 36).

Is not this acknowledgment of the spiritual fatherhood of God, which here prefaces Christ's own employment of prayer, as well as His recommended form for the use of His disciples, another expression of the conception of God as the supreme Spirit of Life, manifested through love, and attested by the Spirit of Truth, which finds representation in His words and deeds and in His rite of communion?

Now, if we assume men's ideas of heaven and hell to be respectively the imagined realisation of desire and the compendium of fear, of a degree and kind consistent with their physical and spiritual evolution, and forming the basis of their prayer to God, an appreciation of the means and end of prayer as advocated by Christ should in some measure reveal His ideas on the subject of human immortality.

The keynote of His reported teaching on prayer is that of union with the Will of God which, held by Him to be the true end of all attempted spiritual correspondence with God, becomes at once the foundation of and the justification for the Christian's hope of immortality.

"Not every one that saith unto me, Lord, Lord, shall enter into the kingdom of heaven; but he that doeth the will of the Father which is in heaven" (St Matt. vii. 21).

Not merely by calling upon the name of Christ, but by obeying His injunction to realise with Him our union with God as the Spirit of Life, and to make our wills one with the Divine Will, is the certainty of our spiritual inheritance revealed to us. For, "This is life eternal, that they might know thee the only true God, and Jesus Christ, whom thou hast sent" (St John xvii. 3).

We know the true God through form, through the expression of God, through the Word, learning from Christ to apprehend the Spirit of Life behind the Name or Manifested Life. "I have manifested thy name unto the men which thou gavest me out of the world.... I have given them the word ... thy word is truth" (St John xvii.).

The mental development of man gives him vantage-ground whence he can, if he will, obtain with a clearness, certainty, and completeness proportionate to the intellectual elevation he has attained, on the one side a retrospective view of his descent, and on the other a perspective discernment of his possible destiny. In other words, the whence of his being is more remotely traceable, and the whither of his evolution more definitely perceptible, according as his growing powers of thought and reason enable him to deduce from his present circumstances certain data bearing on the past history of his life. Knowledge of facts pertaining to his descent, by enlarging his consciousness of himself in his relation to the Whole of Life, offers an explanation of his present status that is at the same time a basis for the forecasting of his future possible fate, testifies to the continuity of his being, and brings his conception of immortality within reasonable bounds of justification.

But confirmation of his ideas of human immortality is dependent upon an ability to attain an intellectual vantage-ground high enough to permit him to trace to its source the history of his life, and to throw a previsionary understanding over the destined end of his evolutionary career, wherein the blending of his physical and spiritual immortality is gradually revealed to him. For in the same way that an examination of the evolution of prayer leads to the observation of a change from specific petition to spiritual acquiescence—a change which we may interpret as evidence of the development of the soul of man, and of the collective consciousness of Creation—so in the study of the life-history of mankind we reach a point whence we may behold the unbroken continuity of his physical evolution merging into that of spiritual evolution. That is to say, the physical immortality of mankind as a whole (the varied manifestation of the Spirit of Life through changing species) is crowned by individual consciousness of spiritual immortality, wherein the purpose of the incarnation of life finds fulfilment.

Pride of ancestry is so prominent a characteristic of nations, families, and individuals alike, that there is some justification for calling it a peculiarity of the human race. Men glory in the possession of records that tell of mighty deeds of valour wrought by their progenitors. Pride of kinship with heroes of past times breeds a sense of responsibility as an accompaniment to the inheritance of a noble name, urging the necessity of passing it on to posterity if not enriched, at least untarnished in its purity.

The idea of the immortality of the individual in the race, characterising the Hebrews as recorded in the Books of the Old Testament, is one outcome of this innate pride of birth, which here becomes, as in many other instances, incorporated as part foundation of a religious creed. Ancestor-worship is another such example. Only, be it noted, whereas this idea of the continuity of being finds its chief expression in recognising and revering the link between present and past generations of men, that of the Hebrew is built upon a conception of survival in their children. Both offer a remarkable testimony to the innate desires of men to contribute towards the continuity of humanity in the establishment of the individual's relationship to the Whole of Life. The Hebrew prays that his seed may multiply and cover the face of the earth, seeing therein the security of his own immortality. But the prayer of a devout Chinaman embodies rather his recognition of honour due to his dead ancestors than his desire to secure a prolific progeny. He is the child of the past, rather than, as the Hebrew, a child of expectancy.

With regard to the ideas of spiritual correspondence embodied in the theories of the transmigration and reincarnation of spirits, it would appear that such are an outcome of the same search after truth that found expression nineteen hundred years ago in the Christian doctrine of the spiritual immortality of all men, by reason of their derivative union with God as the Spirit of Life, and which are to-day confirmed and reincorporated in the scientific theories of the evolutionary descent of man and the unity of Nature.

But it is noteworthy that although the Christian idea of immortality is dissociated from that of the survival of the individual in the race, as well as independent of the belief in the transmigration and reincarnation of spirit in ways other than by the transmission of personality from parents to their children, it is by no means antagonistic to, but rather comprehensive of, all these ideas of the continuity of being. Christ's teaching adequately gathers together the truth in all the scattered and imperfect ideas of spiritual survival latent in the tenets of the religious creeds and theories to which reference has been made. But whereas the Hebrew and Chinese ideas inculcate the keeping apart of races and of nations, with a clinging to past tradition necessarily detrimental to progress; and whereas the transmigration and reincarnation theories constitute a practical annihilation of the survival of individual consciousness,—the Christian conception makes for union among men of all peoples of all times, showing immortality to consist not only in men's relationship to past and future generations of their own race, or by connection with the inter-evolution of other organisms, but also and chiefly in their recognition of God as the supreme Spirit of Life manifested through love, and known to them as the Father of their beings. Perception of this truth establishes union among all men, and gives them consciousness of their assured spiritual and individual immortality.

Thus considered, the Christian idea of human immortality may be seen to be a natural growth from the conception of the survival of the individual in the race. It is as remarkable a testimony to the development of spiritual consciousness, regarded as a whole, as is the evolution of prayer from its form of specific petition to that of spiritual acquiescence. For here again we can perceive how spiritual has accompanied physical evolution—how the evolving apprehension of the soul has kept pace with the confirming comprehension of the mind of man. And here again we see how the doctrine of Christ unites past tradition with new developments of intellectual aspiration, His method of instruction following the perfect order of Nature, wherein nothing is irregular or unreasonable, and whereby the indwelling Spirit of Truth affords perpetual evidence of the development of spiritual consciousness through natural evolution. The changing of the old order is a necessary accompaniment to progress. When Christ announced His mission to be that of fulfilment and not of destruction, was He not inferring the expansion of knowledge physically perceived into apprehension of its spiritual significance—an expansion which, foreseen by Him to be the accompaniment of the future development of man, would call for continual verification by the critical testimony of the Spirit of Truth? The insistence laid by Him upon the necessity of the realisation by men of their spiritual union with God as the basis of all effective prayer, is fully corroborated in His teaching relating to human immortality. Indeed, the whole programme of thought and conduct presented by Him to His disciples can be resolved into an advocacy of prayer as the means of obtaining conscious spiritual union with God, with the attendant purpose of establishing thereby the conviction of spiritual immortality. For eternal life is perceived to be the natural inheritance of all who through prayer have established correspondence with God as the Spirit of Life and the Father of their beings, and who therefore know themselves to be partakers of the infinite and illimitable divinity of God.

Whether we consider the brotherly love between men recommended by Christ as the Will of God; or the self-sacrifice of the individual in the interests of the community, advocated by Him as the foundation of true happiness; or the indwelling Spirit of Life in form, manifested by love in Nature and illustrated in His rite of communion—the same realisation of the kinship of all life follows the putting into practice of His commands, with the result that spiritual life is perceived to be the birthright of all the children of God.

Proof of immortality is thus closely associated with the desire to correspond with the Will of God, for through prayer is the Divine Spirit of Life made visible. Born of the prayers of the faithful expectant, the Manifested Deity is the incarnation of the ideal desires of mankind—the accumulated product

of those periods of anticipation which constitute the preparation for fulfilment of desire, and thus make possible some special culminating revelation which shall be adapted to human recognition. If the light of God be in men, shall they not by that light perceive His glory? Designed in the image of God, shall not man become like unto God, according as the divinely implanted desire to know God shall lead him towards a more perfect correspondence with His Will?

All revelations of God are representative also of the spiritual progress of mankind. The cultivation of qualities considered admirable in human conduct must be preliminary to the evolution of that type of humanity which shall be capable of appreciating as a divine manifestation the incarnation of certain desired spiritual attributes which are conceived of as partaking of the nature of God.

The Kingdom of God is within us. Therefore must the manifested Divinity be born of the prayers of the devout. Thus only can God be made visible to men. Thus only can His Kingdom be established as heaven on earth. And thus do we learn to regard immortality as the fulfilment of prayer. For since the spiritual progress of mankind is achieved and sustained by an increasing consciousness of the glory of God, men must worship as the manifested Divinity of God the embodiments of those spiritual qualities which represent the ideals of their own desire. Therefore, to bring about the conscious and willing co-operation of Creation with the progressive Will of Love, we have first earnestly to desire the coming of the Kingdom of God, which desire shall be the preparation for our enlightenment, when the pure in heart shall see God. His Kingdom is here at hand, shaping in the midst of us, not approaching from afar as a condemnatory judgment upon our imperfections, but as the increasing revelation of Divine Love—a manifestation which is at once our judgment and our joy. For from the beginning the Word of God, the absolute Truth of God, has been one with His divine glory; and from the beginning the progressive consciousness of Creation has been guided by the revelation of the Will of Love and sustained by the Spirit of Truth.

Therefore, if language be the sign of thought, making for progressive union of men, and thereby promoting the growth of spiritual consciousness; and form be evidence of spirit, productive through love of continuity of the manifestation of spirit; and Nature be the vesture of God, wherein the intercommunion of all God's creatures is shown to rest upon mutual sacrifice for mutual continuity of being—is not the incarnate purpose of all these things the attainment by men of conscious union and co-operation with their God?

www.ingramcontent.com/pod-product-compliance
Lightning Source LLC
Chambersburg PA
CBHW081627100526

44590CB00021B/3639